War in our time

T5-DGY-844

War in our time: Reflections on Iraq, terrorism and weapons of mass destruction

Ramesh Thakur

United Nations University Press

TOKYO · NEW YORK · PARIS

© United Nations University, 2007

The views expressed in this publication are those of the author and do not necessarily reflect the views of the United Nations University.

United Nations University Press
United Nations University, 53-70, Jingumae 5-chome,
Shibuya-ku, Tokyo 150-8925, Japan
Tel: +81-3-3499-2811   Fax: +81-3-3406-7345
E-mail: sales@hq.unu.edu   general enquiries: press@hq.unu.edu
http://www.unu.edu

United Nations University Office at the United Nations, New York
2 United Nations Plaza, Room DC2-2062, New York, NY 10017, USA
Tel: +1-212-963-6387   Fax: +1-212-371-9454
E-mail: unuona@ony.unu.edu

United Nations University Press is the publishing division of the United Nations University.

Cover design by Rebecca S. Neimark, Twenty-Six Letters

Printed in India

ISBN 978-92-808-1145-2

Library of Congress Cataloging-in-Publication Data

Thakur, Ramesh Chandra, 1948–
War in our time : reflections on Iraq, terrorism and weapons of mass
destruction / Ramesh Thakur.
    p.   cm.
 Includes bibliographical references and index.
 ISBN 978-9280811452 (pbk.)
 1. Terrorism. 2. War on Terrorism, 2001– 3. Iraq War, 2003– 4. Weapons of
mass destruction. I. Title.
HV6431.T562   2007
973.931—dc22   2007009549

Contents

Introduction

Like the Vietnam War in the 1960s, the Iraq war is likely to be the defining issue that will shape the contours of world politics in the initial decades of the 21st century. It called into sharp relief many fundamental questions about the circumstances when force may justly be used overseas; when, to what degree and for how long, civil liberties and human rights may be curtailed in defence of national security; the extent to which international law may be set aside in pursuit of new age criminals like international terrorists; the wisdom of preemptive and preventive wars to forestall the acquisition of weapons of mass destruction by outlaw regimes and nonstate actors; and the lawfulness and legitimacy of organizing international action outside the framework of the established institutions of global governance centred on the United Nations.

By the end of 2006, most Americans had rejoined the mainstream of international opinion in believing that the Iraq war was a mistake and not worth the cost in lives, American as well as Iraqi, and money. Their main interest was in how best to extricate the United States with the least resulting damage in the Middle East and to global US interests. This was reflected in the mid-term Congressional elections and then in the report of the bipartisan Iraq Study Group chaired by James Baker and Lee Hamilton. For many international commentators, the wonder was that it took Americans so long to wake up to the damage inflicted on the image, prestige and interests of the United States by a war of choice that was widely viewed as misconceived at best and mendacious at worst.

Yet a clear majority of Americans had supported the administration in going after Saddam Hussein in 2003. The main intellectual and moral warrant was provided by an influential cast of intelligentsia who collectively came to be known as humanitarian warriors: an odd marriage of values and power between liberal internationalists who wanted to protect foreign citizens from atrocities perpetrated by their own governments and neoconservatives who believed in exercising American might internationally to protect American interests and project American values around the globe. When the Iraq adventure ran into a sandy quagmire, many public intellectuals who had been the chief cheerleaders blamed the outcome on flawed post-war plans for occupation, negligent mismanagement and criminal incompetence. Some even concluded that the Iraqis were not worthy of the lives and treasure expended by the Americans to liberate them from Saddam Hussein's tyranny and offer them the gift of US-style democracy.

This is disingenuous. The Iraq tragedy was richly foretold, by the millions who marched on the streets against the war before it began as well as by the governments which refused to join the narrow coalition of the willing who actually waged war. The honour roll of sceptical dissenters also included a few Americans, from William Pfaff of *The International Herald Tribune* to Paul Krugman writing in *The New York Times*. Uniquely in the 62-year history of the United Nations, I was given the latitude to write for public consumption on the contested topics of the day, making it clear that I was expressing my personal opinion. This collection brings together my writings on the set of issues associated with the raging debates over the Iraq war from the time of the terrorist attacks of 11 September 2001 until the end of 2006. All but one were written for newspapers in Australia, Canada, Japan and India as well as *The International Herald Tribune*. The exception is the article published in the *United Nations Chronicle*, written jointly with Hans van Ginkel, Rector of the United Nations University (my boss). My time with the United Nations happened to coincide more or less with Kofi Annan's tenure and included a stint working for his second reform report. The collection ends with my tribute to him to mark the completion of his remarkable tenure as Secretary-General of the United Nations.

I begin with three scene-setting articles. The first is the destruction of the Bamiyan statues in Afghanistan in early 2001. There are two reasons for starting with this. It shows that the nature of the Taliban regime was well-known even before 9/11. And it makes the point that the destructive use to which religions' definition of "the other" can be put is not limited to Islamic fundamentalists. Of all my published material, this is the only one that identified my religious affiliation. The next article is a reflection on the paradox of why wars persist despite the almost universal yearning for peace. And the third is an article written in the immediate aftermath of 9/11 that stands the test of time rather well. It is possible to combine intellectual toughness, moral clarity and an international social conscience, after all.

There is, in the collection, the occasional light-hearted article. But by and large the subject matter does not permit much levity and the issues are discussed and analyzed dispassionately and soberly. The events which prompted them are already history. But the issues discussed are important and retain a freshness and contemporary plus future relevance.

I am grateful to the publications concerned for permission to reprint the articles in this collection. While some of the material from the original versions has been removed in order to eliminate any duplication and repetition, and the language and style has been standardized to meet UNU Press guidelines, all relevant articles have been included, and no article has been modified by so much as a single word to realign it with subsequent events or interpretations.

1

Vandalism in Afghanistan and no one to stop it

The International Herald Tribune, 6 March 2001

The world has watched the destruction of Afghanistan's Buddha statues with impotent horror. Among the outraged spectators is the Bharatiya Janata Party government of India. The party's ideological extremists destroyed the 400-year-old mosque in Ayodhya in December 1992. One wonders if they see the parallel.

The barbarism of the Taliban Islamic militia in Afghanistan seems to know no bounds. After placing most of Afghanistan under the harshest rule, the Pakistan-backed Taliban is now setting out to destroy Afghanistan's historical treasures and identity.

Its reclusive and faceless leader, Mullah Mohammed Omar, who has hardly ventured anywhere beyond his sanctuary in the southern Afghan city of Kandahar and parts of Pakistan and has not been photographed to date, has issued the order for the destruction of all "statues" as "un-Islamic." His main target is a 1,500-year-old statue of the Buddha in the central Afghan province of Bamiyan. This 53-metre-high sculpture, carved into a cliff face, is the most famous landmark in Afghanistan and the most visible testimony to the country's Buddhist past before the arrival of Islam in the ninth century. It is one of the few historical treasures to have survived the country's turbulent and violent history.

The statue happens to be located in the province that has traditionally housed the Afghan Shiite Muslim minority, which has been a target of the Taliban's Sunni sectarian hatred. The Taliban took over the province in 1998. In the last few months Bamiyan has changed hands several times between the Taliban and the opposition. Since 1998 the Taliban has threatened to destroy the Buddha statue and its subsidiaries, and has carried out horrific massacres of the province's Shiite inhabitants. But not until now did the Taliban leader issue the specific order for destruction of the statues. This comes at a time of mounting failure to crush all opposition to the Taliban's barbaric rule in the name of Islam. There is frustration, too, at failure to gain international recognition as the legitimate government of Afghanistan.

The destruction of pre-Islamic statues ought to prove counterproductive. It is important that the international community stand firm against this act of the Taliban. There is nothing in Islam that could justify the destruction of history and culture. Islam is a rich religion that aims to enlighten its followers about their past and to guide them to a bright future. It shares with Buddhism an emphasis on enlightened compassion and tolerance. The most important aesthetic quality of all statues of the Buddha is serenity.

In India, meanwhile, a group of militants has been determined to prove that Hindus can match the Taliban in discrediting a great religion. Having destroyed the 16th century mosque eight years ago, religious nationalists now embarrass the nation by attacking Christians for being un-Indian. The political payoff to the Bharatiya Janata Party comes from attention being drawn to Sonia Gandhi's Italian Catholic background. The party is committed to refashioning the Indian polity in the image of "Hinduness." Party candidates ask voters to choose between "Rome rule" and "Rama rule," Rama being one of the main Hindu gods and "Rama rule" being a popular metaphor for an idealized state of affairs. Like the Taliban, the Hindu extremist movement draws vitality from a reaction to the perceived evils of foreign cultural imperialism. In the name of cultural purity, they engage in cultural vandalism of the most primitive sort.

To destroy history is to erase collective identity. The Bamiyan Buddha was as much a part of every Afghan's cultural treasure as the Taj Mahal, an Islamic monument and still a functioning mosque, is part of every Hindu's cultural inheritance.

For 1,500 years the Buddha smiled down to travellers on the great Silk Road. One of those was Babur, founder of the Mughal empire, after whom the 16th century mosque in Ayodhya was named. Truly the statues were a common heritage of mankind. Now they are disappearing.

Who has responsibility for protecting humanity's common heritage? How can we hold cultural criminals accountable for their acts of desecration and destruction?

Note

Article co-authored by Amin Saikal and Ramesh Thakur. Mr. Saikal, a Muslim from Afghanistan, is a professor of political science and director of the Centre for Arab and Islamic Studies at the Australian National University in Canberra. Mr. Thakur, a Hindu from India, is vice-rector of the United Nations University in Tokyo.

2

Why peace exceeds our grasp

The Globe and Mail, 14 July 2001

In the Middle East, the Israeli-Palestinian flare-up worsens by the week. The tortuous search for peace in Kashmir keeps falling into treacherous crevasses on the Himalayas. In Korea dark clouds blot out any silver lining from the occasional sunshine policy. The roots of all three go back to the immediate aftermath of the Second World War.

Is conflict the normal condition of human society and peace the exception? Many contemporary conflicts are peculiarly resistant to resolution because contradictory logics tilt the balance towards their perpetuation.

While most conflicts today are internal wars, almost all international modalities are designed for interstate warfare. The formal authority for maintaining international security lies with the United Nations. But the facts of power place the burden of leadership on the United States. Constantly warned against acting as the world policeman, Uncle Sam is the first cop on the beat to get the distress call whenever there is a mugging anywhere in the global neighbourhood. Today Americans are being urged to stay the course in the Balkans, re-engage with the Middle East peace process, get actively involved in Kashmir, and endorse Seoul's dialogue with North Korea.

The reality of increasing internationalization and globalization collides against the persistence of competitive nationalisms. In Kashmir the secular nationalism of India competes with the religious nationalism of Pakistan and the ethnic nationalism of Kashmiris. In the Balkans all attempts to preserve and recreate a modern multiethnic society fall victim to vicious medieval tribalism.

To resolve a conflict, we must recognize that there are at least two parties, both with elements of right and wrong, and the need for flexibility and pragmatism that permits compromise and accommodation. National or religious zealotry fights against all of this.

The logics of the past and future can be at war. For the sake of a future of peaceful coexistence, communities need to jettison their historical baggage of hatreds. But, because myths are important in the social construction of political identity, history is a fiercely contested terrain. How can one be a Jew today without internalizing the collective consciousness of the Holocaust? Palestinians believe that the refusal of their right to repatriation is an attempt to deny their collective history and identity.

The logic of power is inconsistent with that of justice. Peace in the Middle East or the subcontinent cannot be grasped without bending to the military superiority of Israel and India. But no peace agreement will last if it is fundamentally unjust, resting on the temporary inability of the territorially revisionist Palestinians and Kashmiris to challenge the entrenched might of the status quo powers.

The logic of negotiation tends to be contradictory. The stronger see no reason to compromise. Israeli voters privileged the security of the ingroup over justice for the out-group. The weaker fear that negotiations, if not delayed until parity or superiority has been attained, will force them into humiliating sell-outs of their cause. The Palestinians felt that the offer tabled at Camp David last year was made on the assumption of their military weakness: they seek justice in full, not the crumbs of charity. But what of historically-informed justice for Jews?

The logics of peace and justice are contradictory. Peace is forward-looking, problem-solving and integrative, requiring reconciliation between past enemies within an inclusive community. Justice is backward-looking, finger-pointing and retributive, requiring trial and punishment of the perpetrators of past crimes. Is it possible to move forward without confronting and overcoming the past? Will the pursuit of human rights violators delay and impede efforts to establish conditions of security so that displaced people can return home and live in relative peace once again? The tension must be reconciled on a case-by-case basis rather than on a rigid formula. And it is best resolved by the countries concerned, whether Chile, South Africa, Indonesia or Northern Ireland, not by outsiders. Europeans in particular must resist the temptation to embark on a new wave of judicial colonialism.

The democratic peace thesis holds that democracies do not go to war against one another. Yet some of the best established democracies are among the most involved in warfare. Leaders who might be inclined to negotiate peace can be held back by fear of electoral consequences or destroyed for their daring. Ehud Barak offered more to the Palestinians than was conceivable even a year ago. Ariel Sharon went to Temple Mount in September, provoked a Palestinian uprising, the downfall of Barak and his own election as prime minister. Would an elected leader of India or Pakistan dare to make concessions to the enemy when political rivals are waiting in the wings to ridicule and exploit any "sellout"?

The moment for making peace may not be the most propitious for forging a consensus or political will among the relevant actors to make the necessary decisions and compromises. Human history is full of missed opportunities. But there may be good political reasons why these opportunities could not be grasped at their most opportune. Arafat missed his moment at Camp David last July: he simply could not have sold that package to his Palestinian people and fellow-Arabs at that time. For the first time in fifty years, India is showing signs of willingness to engage in a peace process in Kashmir. But the political, economic and religious mix in Pakistan remains inauspicious for achieving liftoff.

The final contradiction is between war as the historical method of settling conflicts and its present illegitimacy. The logic of force is essentially escalatory. It is difficult to impress upon nationalistically inflamed passions the enormous disparity between the ends sought, the means used, and the price paid. Milosevic's decade-long quest for Greater Serbia is the perfect metaphor for the gap between goals, means and results.

3

An international perspective on global terrorism

United Nations Chronicle 38:3 (2001), pp. 71–73

On Tuesday, 11 September, global terrorism struck in the homeland and at the headquarters of globalization. The history of United States international involvement could be split along the dividing line of the attacks: the age of innocence before; and the fallen world of post-modern terror after. No one can condone the terrorist attacks, and we wish to extend our deepest condolences to all families who lost loved ones in the tragedy. As part of coming to terms with the trauma, it is important that we in the global academic community look at the civilizational imperatives, and challenge, in our collective fight against terrorism.

What do the terrorists want? To divide the West from the Arab and Islamic world, to provoke disproportionate and merciless retaliation that will create a new generation of radicalized terrorists, and to destroy the values of freedom, tolerance and the rule of law. More than anything else, they want to polarize the world into hard divisions, to break harmony into strife, to replace the community of civilized countries with the flames of hatred between communities. They must not be allowed to succeed.

In their insular innocence – and, in the views of some, in their insolent exceptionalism – Americans had embraced the illusion of security behind supposedly impregnable lines of continental defence. To be sure, the United States too had suffered acts of terror – but not as a daily fear, an everyday reality, a way of life that has become commonplace in so many other countries over the past few decades. And no one, anywhere, had suffered terrorist carnage on such a devastating, mind-numbing scale.

Osama bin Laden's evil genius has been to fuse the fervour of religious schools (madrassas), the rallying power of the call to holy war (jihad), the cult of martyrdom through suicide (shahid), the reach of modern technology and the march of globalization into the new phenomenon of global terrorism.

Although the monuments to American power and prosperity were shaken to their foundations, the foundation of a civilized discourse among the family of nations must not be destroyed. Responses that are crafted must be carefully thought out and their consequences fully thought through, with a balance between retaliatory counter-measures and long-term resolution, and bearing in mind the lessons, among others, of the involvement of the British and Soviet empires in Afghanistan, the Germans in the Balkans and the Americans themselves in Vietnam. The rhetoric and metaphors of frontier justice from the days of the Wild West in the United States, or from the time of the Crusades, may rouse domestic fervour but also fracture the fragile international coalition.

Like the two world wars, the "war" against terrorism is one from which America can neither stay disengaged nor win on its own, nor one that can be won without full US engagement.

America has been the most generous nation in the world in responding to emergencies and crises everywhere else. Now that the attack has happened in their heartbreak-land, Americans should be heartened by the spontaneous, warm and overwhelming response from everyone else. The world has grieved and suffered and mourned along with Americans as one.

Nevertheless, the rhetoric of "war" is fundamentally misleading for many reasons: no state is the target of military defeat, there are no uniformed soldiers to fight, no territory to invade and conquer, no clear defining point that will mark victory. The border between "global terrorism" and global organized crime has become increasingly tenuous. In many important respects, terrorism is a problem to be tackled by law-enforcement agencies, in cooperation with military forces; its magnitude can be brought down to "tolerable" levels, but it can never be totally "defeated," just as we cannot have an absolutely crime-free society; and it is part of the growing trend towards the lowered salience of the state in the new security agenda that emphasizes human as well as national security.

The world is united in the demand that those responsible for the atrocities of that tragic Tuesday must be found and brought to justice, but the innocent must be spared further trauma. All allies and many others have already expressed full support, which has been warmly welcomed by Washington. This should encourage and help Washington to re-engage with the global community on the broad range of issues, not disengage still more through in-your-face rejections of international regimes. Global cooperation is not a one-way street: the relationship requires long-term commitment on all sides.

The global coalition to combat threats to international security, of any type, is already in place. We call it the United Nations. It did not rate a mention in the American president's address to the joint session of Congress. There is a fresh opportunity to rededicate the terms of American engagement with the international community in protecting the world from deadly new threats immune to conventional tools of statecraft. The nation of laws must turn its power to the task of building a world ruled by law. An order that is worth protecting and defending must rest on the principles of justice, equity and law that are embedded in universal institutions.

President George W. Bush has declared that the United States will make no distinction between terrorists and those who harbour them. Nor must Washington make a distinction between "our" terrorists and "theirs," condoning or tolerating one lot while isolating and liquidating another. For security from the fear of terrorism is truly indivisible. How many of today's radical extremists, embracing terror against a host of countries, are yesterday's "freedom fighters" trained and financed by the West as jihadis against the former enemy? Are there more to follow, more to be created? How interconnected is the terrorists' network, how overlapping their cause? Washington must not fall into the trap, only too distressingly common in their past, of converting terror on America into terror against the world, but terrorist attacks elsewhere are seen merely as local problems to be solved by the countries concerned. It is worth highlighting that around 40 percent of the World Trade Center victims were non-Americans from 80 countries: it really was an international tragedy.

Fundamentalism infects aspects of US contemporary policy in ways that form the backdrop to the tragedy of 9/11. On one side, fundamentalist belief in limited government produced policies of privatizing even such critical public goods as airport security in the hands of poorly paid, ill-trained airport screeners. There are some services that properly belong to the public sector, including citizens' health, education, public safety, and law and order. There is a fundamentalist drive to promote the rule of the market in international transactions, regardless of the social consequences and oblivious of the darkening storm clouds on the horizon. And there is a fundamentalist opposition to institutions of global governance, from arms control to climate change and the pursuit of universal justice – justice without borders.

The events of that tragic Tuesday should force us to rethink old and set ways of looking at the world. In the war against fundamentalist terrorism, past enemies can be today's allies. The concert of democracies must cooperate politically and coordinate responses with one another's law-enforcement and military forces. They must forge alliances if necessary to work around the institutionalized reluctance of global organizations to respond effectively and in time to real threats instead of posturing over imaginary grievances.

Security experts will examine closely the procedural and organizational flaws that allowed the planes to be hijacked and the intelligence failures that enabled it all to be plotted without detection. Other security measures will also be put in place. But in the end there can be no guaranteed security against suicide terrorists who know no limits to their audacity, imagination and inhumanity. We must not privilege security and order to such an extent as to destroy our most cherished values of liberty and justice in the search for an unattainable absolute security. As Benjamin Franklin, one of the fathers of American independence, said, those who would sacrifice essential liberty to temporary safety deserve neither liberty nor safety.

In looking for underlying causes, Americans should ask why they arouse such fanatic hatred in would-be terrorists. Is all of it the price they have to pay for being the world's most successful, powerful and wealthy nation? Or can some of it at least be muted by adopting policies that are more measured and tempered in dispensing justice more evenly? Fanaticism feeds on grievance, and grievance is nurtured by deeply felt injustice. Terror is the weapon of choice of those who harbour the sense of having been wronged, who are too weak to do anything about it through conventional means, and who are motivated to seek vengeance by other means.

Whatever else they may have been, the suicide terrorists responsible for that Tuesday's attacks were not cowards. On the contrary, they were exceptional in their steel of resolve, even if it was harnessed to an evil end. Random acts by individual terrorists can be sourced to the politics of collective grievance: dehumanizing poverty and spirit-sapping inequality, as well as group injustice.

President Bush spoke of an "unyielding anger" in his first broadcast to the nation. Such human emotions are not exceptional to one people but common to the human race. The fury and vengeance of others fester in deeply wounded collective psyche: if we wrong them, shall they not revenge? Anger is a bad guide to policy, for governments as for terrorists: revenge is indeed a dish best served cold.

Terrorism cannot be contained by expensive space-based shields against missile attacks. Modern military forces and security policies should be configured for threats rooted in the new security agenda, but bearing in mind that at the end of the day, it is simply not possible to construct and keep in place indefinitely foolproof protective shields against every threat.

If isolationism is not an option in today's interconnected world, unilateralism cannot be the strategy of choice either. Just as America is a nation of laws that find expression in institutions, so Americans should work to construct a world of laws functioning through international institutions.

That is why the concert of democracies to combat terrorism cannot be a closed circle, but must embrace all those willing to join in the fight against threats to a civilized community of nations. A global coalition formed to combat terrorism must not be restricted to punitive and retributive goals, but must instead be transformed into the larger cause of rooting security worldwide in enduring structures of cooperation for the longer term. The supremacy of the rule of law has to be established at the national, regional and global levels. The principles of equity and justice must pervade all institutions of governance.

Americans rightly reject moral equivalence between their own "virtuous" power and their "evil" enemies. They should now reflect on their own propensity towards political ambivalence between the perpetrators of terrorism and the efforts of legitimate governments to maintain national security and assure public safety.

The end of complacency about terrorism in the American heartland should encourage Washington to view other countries' parallel wars against terrorism through the prism of a fellow-government facing agonizing policy choices in the real world, rather than single-issue nongovernmental organizations, whose vision is not anchored in any responsibility for policy decisions. Some governments have been at the receiving end of moral and political judgment about robust responses to violent threats posed to their authority and order from armed dissidents. They are entitled to and should now expect not a free hand but a more mature understanding – an understanding forged in the crucible of shared suffering.

This does not give any government a licence to kill. To defeat the terrorists, it is absolutely critical that the symbolism of America – not just the home of the free and the land of the brave, but also the bastion of liberty, freedom, equality between citizens and rulers, democracy and a nation of laws – be kept alive. That is a shared vision. That is why we were all the symbolic target of the attacks, why we were all Americans that Tuesday, and why we must join forces with the Americans to rid succeeding generations of the scourge of terrorism – not blinded by hatred and a lust for revenge, nor driven by the calculus of geopolitical interests, but ennobled by the vision of a just order and empowered by the majesty of laws.

For the sake of our common future, we must not allow reason to be overwhelmed by grief and fear, judgment to be drowned in shock and anger at the terrorist action – as President Bush has affirmed, we must not brand all followers of any particular faith our common enemy. Just as there coexist many ways of thinking and many different value systems within the "West," so are there many who daily honour Islam against the tiny minority who sometimes dishonour it or any other religion.

In the immediate aftermath of the assaults, some have sought to resurrect the vacuous and discredited thesis of the clash of civilizations. Incidents have been reported where members of particular ethnic or religious groups going about their daily lives – shop owners, passers-by – were randomly accused of being responsible for the devastation in New York and Washington, and sometimes assaulted with deadly violence, simply because of their race, colour, religion or attire.

Individual terrorism should not provoke mass intolerance. The victims of the hijacked planes and the World Trade Center destruction, along with the rescuers, reflect modern American society in all its glorious diversity. The best way to honour victims is to recognize our common humanity and work for peace in and through justice. Islamic terrorists are no more representative of Islam than any fundamentalist terrorists are of their broader community: the Irish terrorists (or for that matter some US-based reverends) of Christianity, or the fanatics who in 1992 destroyed the centuries-old mosque in Ayodhya of Hinduism.

The world will fall into a permanent state of suspicion, fear, perhaps even war, if we fail to make a distinction between fanatics, with a total disregard for life, who pose a threat to all of humankind – irrespective of religion, culture or ethnicity – and those who simply have different ways of organizing their lives or different cultural preferences, but share the same basic goals and aspirations of all mankind: the pursuit of life, liberty and happiness.

The need for a dialogue among civilizations is now greater than before, not less. Those whose vision rises above the obvious differences between ethnic, religious, cultural and social groups, and embraces so much that we all have in common, will not judge a human being simply on a person's looks, language and faith. This is what the dialogue among civilizations is about.

It will take time and effort to bear fruit and certainly, in the short term, will not be able to prevent atrocities like the ones just witnessed. In the long run, however, dialogue might do just that: by uniting those who strive for a common future, and thereby isolating those who want to generate ineradicable rifts between the peoples of the world. America has called on all to stand up and be counted in the war against global terrorism. We do indeed need a worldwide coalition against such horrors.

However, it is just as important to stand up and resist all who would spread the message of hate and sow the seeds of discord.

The fight against terrorism is a war with no frontiers, against enemies who know no borders and have no scruples. If we abandon our scruples, we descend to their level. The dialogue of civilizations is a discourse across all frontiers, embracing communities who profess and practice different faiths, but have scruples about imposing their values on others. We must talk to and welcome into the concert of civilized communities believers in moral values from all continents, cultures and faiths. The need of the hour is for discourse among the civilized, not a dialogue of the uncivilized deafened by the drumbeats of war.

Note

Article co-authored with Hans van Ginkel. Mr. van Ginkel is rector of the United Nations University in Tokyo.

4

Faults of the most benign world power

The Japan Times, 3 October 2001

Responses to the trauma of the terrorist attacks in the United States have covered a broad front in several phases. The most immediate was to institute new security procedures for flying and intensified surveillance of suspected would-be terrorists. This was quickly followed by freezing assets of individuals and organizations linked to suspected terrorist outfits. The next phase will be coordinated military strikes at training camps, bases and perhaps other facilities.

The more difficult part will come later – in eradicating the infrastructure of international terrorism, on the one hand, and addressing the structural grievances that feed the causes of terrorism, on the other. Americans should reflect on why their concentration of power has caused unease outside "Fortress America."

For the record, it should be noted that by historical standards the behaviour of the United States as a great power has been the most benign, bar none. What other great power has a better record of dealing with smaller states, especially smaller neighbours? It would be interesting to know, for example, how many Mexicans would have exchanged their geography for that of Poland over the last two centuries. That said, it is still fair to say that concerns have grown that the United States has become isolationist, unilateralist, exceptionalist and triumphalist.

Isolationism means disengagement from the rest of the world community, retreating to within one's own secure borders and territory. An isolationist US president would not travel abroad and would not send delegates abroad to protect and promote American points of view. The US was essentially isolationist until the 20th century, uninterested in the world beyond the Americas.

Unilateralism refers to a country's acting entirely on its own, based on national interests, preferences and values. Views of other countries might have a bearing on the action chosen but do not determine it. The decision by the Bush administration to withdraw from the Kyoto Protocol is an example.

Internationalism is the opposite of isolationism. It is possible to act as an internationalist and a unilateralist simultaneously – if, for example, the United States decides on its own to take action in Grenada, Haiti, Nicaragua or Iran.

Exceptionalism is the belief that the United States is uniquely blessed and endowed and selfless in international engagement and, therefore, should not be held accountable to standards set for other nations. Exceptionalism may underpin both unilateral and multilateral behaviour. An example of the latter is the idea that the United States has the right to be on the UN Human Rights Commission, since the commission was the brainchild of Eleanor Roosevelt and the United States is the champion promoter of human rights around the world. An example of exceptionalism underpinning unilateralist behaviour is US bombing of alleged terrorist training bases in Afghanistan in retaliation for terrorist attacks on US targets in other countries.

Triumphalism is exultation in national victories and superiority. It is predicated on the belief that the US political and economic model (political values, human rights, rule of law, limited government, the presidential version of representative democracy and the market economy) is, a priori, the best in the world and should be adopted by everyone else.

Because of a sustaining belief that it is a virtuous power, the United States is averse to domesticating international values and norms with respect to greenhouse gas emissions, the death penalty, landmines or the pursuit of universal justice. Because of structural power attributes, the United States, instead, internalizes many of the benefits and externalizes many of the costs of globalization.

US global dominance of military might, economic dynamism and information technology makes it the world's supreme power. The US military budget is greater than that of all other North Atlantic Treaty Organization members combined, accounting for 63 percent of NATO's total budget. Washington also enjoys a unique confluence of advantages for institutionalizing its preferences:

- The ability to overwhelm the negotiating capacities of smaller countries because of the sheer size, depth and range of the US foreign policy bureaucracy

- Hegemony in major multilateral institutions such as the International Monetary Fund and the World Bank
- Collective-action dominance of the Group of Seven nations and NATO
- A much greater scientific-technical depth of knowledge, which is especially useful when negotiations involve complex questions of contested science – as in the subject of global warming
- Superior ability to leverage information and knowledge in pursuing narrow commercial and strategic interests
- Greater capacity to leverage legal resources, enabling the United States to field a formidable team of technically skilled legal specialists in any branch of law
- Advantages of wealth, enabling the United States to exact preemptive compliance by threatening to deny others access to its vast market (it is rich enough to bribe those poor enough to be bribable)
- Immeasurable capacity to deploy national assets such as intelligence to monitor compliance by others
- The fact that it is home to most of the internationally influential media and nongovernmental organization conglomerates

Other countries fret that the post-Cold War era rapidly turned into a unipolar moment and that fitful US arrogance has turned into habitual exceptionalism and triumphalism. Supreme power is viewed as having encouraged the United States to set the rules of globalization: choosing some parts (trade liberalization) while rejecting others (globalized decision-making), lecturing others on the rule of law while refusing to accept international criminal jurisdiction, promoting pluralism and diversity when the world is concerned about the concentration of multimedia power in the United States, etc.

The same country that was founded in opposition to tyranny, that institutionalized this opposition by creating a form of government based on separation of powers and that went on to acquire the most concentrated power ever in world affairs now has difficulty comprehending why others worry about the tyranny of total power. Yet, in today's interconnected world, total power is not enough to guarantee invulnerability to overseas-based threats.

5

Multilateralism is in America's interest

The Japan Times, 6 October 2001

On issues of global warming and the Kyoto Protocol on climate change; weapons of mass destruction and the Anti-Ballistic Missile Treaty, the Comprehensive Test Ban Treaty and the warfare inspection treaties; and the new small-arms control pact, the administration of US President George W. Bush soon pulled back from multilaterally negotiated agreements.

The United Nations is the product, symbol and forum of globalism. The United States is not a modest power and has much to be immodest about. Modesty is a more becoming social skill. In the Persian Gulf War, the UN framework enabled America to avoid the destiny of becoming a hyperpower, engaged and entangled everywhere. Success in the war and in having mobilized the international community to its strategic ends generated triumphalism.

Washington is increasingly viewed as not understanding that the United Nations exists to protect international peace and security – not to project US national interests and globalize American values. Where Americans bemoan UN ineffectualness in bringing to heel rogue states, even sympathetic foreign observers despair at the US tendency to behave like an errant superpower, responsible only to Congress and voters.

Americans see their country as the virtuous power, and define their international role accordingly. Being the virtuous power, the United States, and no one else, has the moral standing and the material capacity to provide international leadership and galvanize the United Nations into action.

The US had no peer competitor in the drafting and construction of the normative architecture of the multilateral machinery for the maintenance of international peace and security. Precisely because they are the most powerful and privileged, the preeminent powers of any system have the biggest stake in that system and the most to lose if it collapses under challenge by the system's territorially, politically, ideologically or economically revisionist members.

The big powers were able to translate their preferences and values into the founding principles, structures and processes of the United Nations to a far greater extent and degree than the small states. In the series of conferences and negotiating sessions that established the United Nations, the smaller states succeeded in securing some concessions to their interests; but the essential machinery was still designed by and for the major powers, especially the United States, Britain and the Soviet Union. The veto clause was inserted to ensure that the United Nations would never construct a global interest in conflict with the national interest of any one of the "permanent five."

Nor does the United States have a peer competitor in operating and driving the UN multilateral machinery. The United Nations is the forum and instrument for externalizing American values and virtues like democracy, human rights, rule of law and market economy, and embedding them in international institutions. The United Nations is less hostile and inimical to US interests than commonly supposed. After the terrorist attacks of 11 September, condemnation by the UN secretary-general was immediate. In addition, within 48 hours the Security Council and the General Assembly had also condemned the attacks and voted to take action against those responsible and any states who aid, support or harbour them.

The United Nations helps the United States mute the costs and spread the risks of the terms of international engagement. It is a means of mediating the choice between isolationism – disengagement with the world – and unilateralism, or going it alone; between inaction because of a refusal to be a cop and intervention as the world's only cop. But to maximize these benefits, Washington needs to instil in itself the principle of multilateralism as a norm in its own right: States must do "X" because the United Nations has called for "X," and good states do what the United Nations asks them to do.

On a few issues, US interests will be subordinated to others' conceptions of the global interest, for example, with respect to proscribing antipersonnel landmines, controlling toxic emissions, or institutionalizing processes of international criminal justice in a new world court.

In such cases, the real question for Washington is never simply whether to reject the particular regime with which it disagrees. Rather, the question becomes: how much damage will rejecting any one particular multilateral regime do to other multilateral regimes, to the principle of multilateralism, and, through spillover effects, to other US national interests?

Do American policymakers really believe that they can construct a world in which all others have to obey universal norms and rules that Washington can opt out of whenever, as often, and for as long as it likes – what Richard Haass, Director of the Policy Planning Unit at the State Department, calls "a la carte multilateralism"?

Alternatively, do American policymakers really believe that a world in which every country retreated into unilateralism would be a better guarantee of US national security, now and in the future, than multilateral regimes and universal codes of behaviour?

The United States is the world's indispensable power, the United Nations the world's indispensable institution. The United Nations is simultaneously the embodiment of the virtues of globalism and the instrument through which US-led collective action can be authorized and implemented with the least pain and most gain. Inconsistency and selectivity risk undermining the entire normative architecture of world order, and are likely to prove more damaging to the interests of the United States than of any other nation.

6

Blaming others is no solution

The Japan Times, 29 October 2001

History always repeats itself, noted Karl Marx: the first time as tragedy, the second as farce.

The hijacking of an Indian Airlines flight at the end of 1999 was a tragedy. An innocent passenger's throat was slit and he bled to death, the plane was taken to Kandahar in Afghanistan, and the complicity of the Taliban regime was there for all but the wilfully blind to see. In one of the most craven capitulations ever made in a hijacking, not only were all the hijackers' demands, including the release of Islamic militants from Indian jails, met, but the militants were also escorted to freedom by India's foreign minister. One of them has now been implicated in the trail of money leading to the hijacker-terrorists believed responsible for the 11 September attacks on the World Trade Center.

Then, in October 2001, we had the farce of a hijacking that never was. The Indian government met in crisis session for several hours, official spokesmen were repeating wild rumours with no basis in fact to the press, and India made itself an international laughing stock with no outside help.

That same month, when suicide-terrorists blew up a van outside the state legislature of Kashmir and killed over a dozen people, New Delhi acted with great dispatch and urgency, firing off letters immediately to Washington demanding that the United States brand Pakistan a state sponsor of terrorism.

Incidents such as these highlight a tendency that has become a national pastime and an international embarrassment: constantly blaming someone else and demanding that others do something about one's own problems.

Cannot get a job or a promotion or a seat in Parliament? This cannot be due to your own lack of abilities or application compared to others. It must be due instead to historical discrimination. Let us redress the social injustice by a new law requiring quotas for your caste or religion or gender.

A terrorist outrage in Punjab or Kashmir or Assam? It cannot possibly be due to any injustice in our own policies, or the brutality of our security forces, or the complete incompetence of our law enforcement and intelligence agencies. It must be due solely to the omnipotence of foreign (read Pakistani) agents doing their evil masters' bidding. The persistence of terrorism for two decades is not due to failure of governance in India but to the refusal of the United States and the United Nations to act decisively.

A farcical drama over a hijacking that wasn't? It has nothing to do with the incompetence that pervades the public sector due to the complete politicization of the public service, which corrupts the public-service ethic and makes government services and contracts open to those offering the highest bribe. These things happen. If Pakistan wasn't responsible it should have been: blame it on them. Weren't the nonexistent hijackers overheard demanding route maps for Lahore?

As part of the agenda of promoting "Hinduness" in public life, some Cabinet ministers have been encouraging the adoption of astrology in university syllabuses. Maybe they should encourage courses in victimology instead.

How can one repatriate the notion of responsibility – individual, collective and national? When hijackers' demands are met, it encourages more brazen and brutal acts of terrorism as a means of holding a soft government to ransom. After the 1999 hijacking there was an upsurge in terrorist activity in Kashmir, money and recruits flowed to the cause of militancy, and the morale of militants was boosted while that of the security forces fell through the floor. Either those who had been held in custody were terrorists, in which case they should have been tried and imprisoned if convicted; or they were not, in which case they should not have been held in indefinite custody in the first place.

Outside involvement in the militancy in Kashmir is almost certain. But isn't the main cause of the rise of militancy the history of policy bankruptcy in New Delhi, and the chief cause of its persistence the incompetence and brutality of the security forces? The immediate threat of terrorism is a security problem to be tackled by the military and law-enforcement and intelligence agencies. But in the longer term, neither the United States nor India is exempt from the need to examine the root causes of grievances that give rise to cross-border terrorism.

The failure of the West to see the war on terrorism as a shared cause may be deplorable from a New Delhi-centred perspective. But do Indian policymakers really expect Western leaders to accept extra complications in their single-minded focus on Afghanistan at the moment? New Delhi should also look closer to home with respect to its failure to nurture a broader public constituency among Indians living in the United States. Indian diplomacy is decades out of date in its one-dimensional focus on government-to-government relations.

The history of US energy firm Enron Corp.'s involvement in power generation and distribution in India is another cautionary tale of turning temporary opportunities into lasting irritants. The Dabhol power plant in Maharashtra State, which was meant to be a fast-track project showcasing India's new permissive environment towards foreign investment, ended up bogged down in a legal wrangle between Enron and the state government, resulting in the loss of decade-long opportunity to put India-US relations on solid foundations. (And Indians have the chutzpah to complain of Pakistani skill in seizing a narrow window of opportunity to rebuild a badly soured relationship with Washington.)

Pakistan's predicament post-9/11 should have been a win-win situation for India. If Pakistan decided to cooperate with Washington in eradicating the infrastructure of terrorism from the region (as it seems to be doing so far), the benefits would automatically flow to India. A stable and prosperous Pakistan is very much in India's interest, too. And if Pakistan faltered in its cooperation, India's long-standing charges would be automatically vindicated. It takes skill to have turned this into what appears to be a lose-lose outcome.

7

Brinkmanship, but not war

The Australian, 31 December 2001

13 December was as defining a moment in India as 11 September was in the United States. New Delhi is not in Kashmir but the nation's capital. The targets were lawmakers, including government ministers. The locale was the heart of India's democracy and the seat of its power.

A week after a terrorist attack that left 13 dead, I visited a senior MP in his office in parliament.[1] The atmosphere was heavy with shock, anger and determination. The talk of town and country is war.

India and Pakistan have moved their missiles in menacing confrontation, cancelled leave for troops, ratcheted up the rhetoric of war, curtailed bilateral contacts on a range of issues and instituted other measures designed to underline that relations in the subcontinent are not business as usual. India's policy seems to be designed more for sabre-rattling than calculated war and addressed to three audiences: domestic opinion, Pakistan and the United States.

New Delhi is a prisoner of its past policy errors and belligerent rhetoric about being the victim of Pakistan-based terrorism for 20 years and the need to solve cross-border terrorism on its own because of double standards by others. Most Indians have become contemptuous of their government's softness and fondness for talk over action.

The contrasting reaction of the US government in taking determined action to rid the world of the Taliban and al-Qaeda within three months of 9/11 has been an eye-opener. Now talk of 20 years of fighting terrorism produces scorn and ridicule. If anything, there is some regret that the 13 December attack did not result in casualties among parliamentarians, so that lawmakers paid the price for the rampant corruption, incompetence and misgovernance that ails the Indian body politic.

The net effect was calls for tough action, including war if necessary, to rid the country of the scourge of Pakistan-based terrorism. New Delhi demanded that Pakistan take specific and focussed action against the terrorists based there. Islamabad formally condemned the attack but asked for proof before taking any action. Most provocatively, in a statement that enraged the people and goaded the government into tough measures, Pakistan's official spokesman suggested that the Indian security agencies may have stage-managed the attack in order to discredit Pakistan.

The message to Pakistan therefore was that India finally had had enough and was prepared to pay any price to end cross-border terrorism. The problem is: what exactly will New Delhi do? It lacks the asymmetric military dominance of the United States and Israel vis-a-vis the Taliban and Palestinians. The alleged terrorist camps in Pakistani Kashmir are tent and training affairs, not permanent installations; they can be relocated or replaced with relative ease. Missiles are expensive and ineffectual, as Bill Clinton's strikes against Osama bin Laden showed.

Action against Pakistani air bases would risk striking at US equipment and personnel and, if unexpectedly successful, could provoke a nuclear escalation. Any military operation would unite Pakistanis behind the militants and so undermine the fight against international terrorism.

The Indian government is acutely aware of the dilemma, even if the people are not. Hence the preferred strategy of brinkmanship in order to compel Washington to tighten the screws on Islamabad. But this too is a high-risk strategy. Having firmly rejected outside interference in Kashmir, does New Delhi really want intensified international involvement in the subcontinent's geopolitics?

Because of the historic mistrust of US policies and motives, most Indians seem unable to comprehend that in fact the US war on terror has slowly but surely worked to their security advantage. With the war against the Taliban having been won, Washington's attention is concentrated on Pakistan as the epicentre of global terrorism.

But just as there is increasing acceptance of the reality of de facto Pakistani complicity in harbouring international terrorists, so there is increasing appreciation of the risks of nuclear conflict rooted in the intractable Kashmir dispute. And on this there is less international support for India and more sympathy for Pakistani complaints.

The simplest, least costly and most acceptable solution might be to declare the Line of Control to be the international border. This would legalize the territorial and political status quo and affirm the principle that borders should not be changed by force. Whether the option is acceptable to either India or Pakistan is a different issue. Siblings by geography and history, they are tied too in destiny. Together, they can yet be masters of a shared future of peace and prosperity. Locked in perpetual rivalry, they will remain objects of international intrigue.

Note

1. Dr Manmohan Singh, who subsequently became the prime minister of India.

8

Tackling global terrorism

The Japan Times, 2 February 2002

It is clear now that Afghanistan had been taken hostage by the murderous cabal of the Taliban and al-Qaeda. As the US-supported Northern Alliance liberated the country from the grip of the terrorists, it was interesting to witness the depth of the Afghan people's hatred for the foreign fighters who had taken over their country. The foreign "warriors" had also appropriated many overseas "Islamic" causes under one umbrella. Chants by the Taliban and al-Qaeda fighters often spewed hatred against the United States, Israel and India.

Looking at the recent terrorist attacks in these three countries, it is possible to identify elements that must be addressed in order to "drain the swamp" of terrorism through an integrated and comprehensive strategy.

The final line of defence is preventive national measures in countries that are the targets of attack. This includes robust counter-terrorism intelligence and surveillance efforts by the law enforcement and national security agencies.

Efforts to build effective defences against international terrorism should focus first on countries that harbour or host individuals and groups advocating, financing, arming and otherwise supporting international terrorism. This is where the export of terror can be stopped or contained most effectively and at the least cost.

This means both mobilizing the will and building the capacity of these states to tackle terrorism. Fragile states with frail institutions are the soft underbelly for global terrorism. Terrorists take advantage of porous borders, weak and corrupt law-enforcement forces and limp judicial systems.

An appropriate mix of carrots and sticks is required. The first task is to build the security capacity of countries fighting to liquidate terrorist cells, as with the new government of Afghanistan; and persuading, coaxing or coercing regimes that are tolerant of terrorist cells to confront the menace instead. International patience with such tolerance is rapidly declining. The Bush administration seems to believe that Pakistan is a more worthy example of fighting terrorism than the Palestinian Authority.

Cooperation is needed between national law-enforcement and national security agencies (information and resource sharing, training exchanges, extradition). There must also be bilateral and multilateral regimes for regulating and controlling the in-border production, storage and cross-border transfer of terrorism-related materials, skills and technology.

There has been much controversy with respect to the "root causes of terrorism." The controversy highlights the tension between tackling today's priorities and adopting a holistic approach. The underlying causes of terrorism can be grouped into five categories.

The first includes the lack of democratic institutions and practices, political freedoms and civil liberties. Good governance and the rule of law constrain the arbitrary exercise of power, mediate citizen-state relations and absorb the strains and stresses of political contestation. Too often in the past major powers have indulged and bankrolled despotism and repression. And autocratic regimes all too often flirt with fundamentalism against third countries, only to be consumed by the same flames. The international margins of tolerance of non-democratic regimes are rapidly shrinking.

Democracies legitimize the struggle for power and channel it into the political process and system. The denial of political representation diverts dissent into alternative channels, including militant religions and extremist causes. Sometimes the mosque has been the only alternative rallying point in autocratic regimes.

Terrorism flourishes amid frustration with repressive, inept, self-aggrandizing, uncaring and unresponsive regimes. Authoritarian governments provoke grievance, whereas representative regimes provide safety valves for collective anger.

This applies even to the world's most populous democracy. India's policy in Kashmir has violated much of the admirable commitment to the theory and practice of democracy, pluralism and tolerance in the rest of the country. The alienation and disaffection of many Kashmiris is rooted more in the repeated negation of their political choices by an intrusive and interfering central government in New Delhi, and in the brutal practices of Indian security forces, than in India being a Hindu-majority country.

Second, group grievance rooted in collective injustice against ethnic and religious sects generates anger and armed resistance when the weaker resort to their comparative advantages in so-called asymmetrical warfare. Often the driving force behind fanatic hatred is despair, not deprivation. If relations are based purely on power, with no concession to justice and equity, then peace and stability rest on insecure foundations, on the temporary inability of the revisionists to challenge the entrenched status quo, and not on their acceptance of the status quo as the legitimate order. This is as true of Israel with respect to the Palestinians as of India in Kashmir. Victims cannot be made to give up their right of resistance. The United States becomes the focus of grievance if its arms and policies are seen to be propping up occupying forces.

Third, determined efforts must be made to resolve intractable and long-standing conflicts, including Palestine and Kashmir, that have spawned generations of radicalized populations. It is America's misfortune that it attracts anger both when it gets involved and when it does not. Uncle Sam is always urged not to be the world's policeman, but is always the first cop on the beat to get a call when there is a mugging in the neighbourhood.

Fourth, poverty and destitution can produce feelings of desperation and alienation and thus be an incubator of terrorism. This is where the swamp metaphor is especially apt. True, Osama bin Laden is (or was) a multimillionaire. But it is hard to imagine Palestine, Pakistan and Afghanistan as major recruiting and training bases and safe havens for terrorism if they were middle-class countries. Poverty also detracts from the state capacity to provide universal education through the public sector, resulting in thousands of children going to private religious schools and being taught the cultures of the Koran and the Kalashnikov.

Finally, a dialogue among civilizations will help to promote intercultural harmony and defuse hate-based terrorism. While the efforts by the likes of US President George W. Bush and British Prime Minister Tony Blair to distinguish between true adherents of ancient faiths and terrorists who hijack religions are worthy, others have fallen into the trap of attacking Arabs and Muslims living in their midst. Equally, however, failure by the true leaders of each faith to denounce extremist violence allows a false link between a particular religion and terrorism to become entrenched in many people's minds.

It is easy to denounce the resort to violence and extremism by others. Civic courage requires us to confront those in our own midst who would hijack our beliefs for their violent goals. Political and religious leaders must persevere in denouncing all extremists within their own groups – commentators are already suggesting that the struggle for the soul of Islam will be fought in Pakistan in the coming weeks and months – and reaching out to followers of other faiths.

9

Working for a safer world

The Japan Times, 17 April 2002

"Weapons of mass destruction" (WMD) refer to biological, chemical and nuclear weapons. During a recent three-day conference in Beijing, organized jointly by the United Nations Department of Disarmament Affairs and the Chinese government, it became clear that we have to choose from a menu of four options with regard to WMD: universalization of these weapons through laissez-faire proliferation; the Nuclear Non-Proliferation Treaty's (NPT) solution of haves and have-nots; differentiated proliferation; and universal abolition.

The story goes that a tourist in Ireland stops his car and asks a local villager for directions. "How do I get to 'X' from here," he asks. "If I wanted to get to X, I wouldn't start from here," he is told.

Similarly, with respect to WMD, we can envision the future that we like, and work to bring it about; or we can start from the "real" world here and today, and accept whatever destination it delivers us to in a few years or decades. The strength of conviction underpinning the abolitionists' campaign is the vision of a world free of weapons of mass destruction and their means of delivery.

The terrorist attacks of 9/11 concentrated American minds on potential terrorist threats using WMD. A world in which anyone who could get WMD was allowed to do so would be a far more dangerous place for all, including the United States. No one seriously advocates letting WMD market-forces triumph in order to level the killing fields for the whole world.

In 1968, the world accepted the nuclear apartheid of the NPT. Non-nuclear countries gave up their nuclear-weapons option in return for a deal with the nuclear powers. The latter promised to pursue negotiations in good faith for complete nuclear disarmament and pledged also not to use nuclear weapons against non-nuclear signatories to the NPT. The first treaty obligation has not been honoured by any of the five nuclear powers; the recent Nuclear Posture Review (NPR) suggests that the United States might be prepared to dishonour the second.

Because of changed political sentiments since 1968, because in bio-chemical weapons it is the "rogue states" whose status as de facto pos-sessors would be legitimized, and because of the nuclear powers' failure to honour their side of the NPT bargain, the NPT-type solution of haves and have-nots has no constituency for WMD in general.

The logic of many recent US statements points to the third option. President George W. Bush has repeatedly warned that the United States will not permit the world's most dangerous regimes to get hold of WMD. The leaked NPR confirms that Washington may be targeting specific regimes, not all those who may be pursuing WMD programs. In effect Washington has decided to divide WMD possessors and seekers into US-friendly, US-neutral and US-hostile.

The fourth option is the total elimination of all WMD for all countries, under internationally negotiated, verifiable and universally applicable treaties. We already have this situation – at least in theory – with regard to biological and chemical weapons; what will be required will be the ne-gotiation of a parallel nuclear-weapons convention, plus one dealing with missiles.

This has the merit of non-discrimination, simplicity and comprehen-siveness. But, sadly, it also has the great defect of unreality for the fore-seeable future. The circuit-breaker in the cycle of nuclear powers is the United States. Far from retreating from nuclear weapons, Washington is refining the critical roles that they play in its defence doctrines and strat-egies, as the NPR makes clear. As long as the United States retains them, so will the other nuclear powers.

But can the threshold of nuclear weapons use be lowered, as contem-plated in the NPR, without also lowering the threshold of nuclear prolif-eration? We have recently had threats from Ichiro Ozawa of the Liberal Party that even Japan – the emotional touchstone of antinuclear senti-ment because it remains the only country to have been the victim of nu-clear weapons – could easily make thousands of nuclear weapons, and China should not forget this. While Ozawa mentioned a figure of 3,000–4,000 nuclear warheads, some antinuclear researchers, who have some-times described Japan as a virtual nuclear-weapons power, place the figure as high as 7,000 warheads. This is unlikely to produce a cutback in the Chinese nuclear arsenal.

Thus the only viable option would appear to be a differentiated rather than a universal policy that discriminates between the virtuous and the vile. This seems to be the only way that we can solve the apparent paradox of threatening, as in the NPR, to use one type of WMD to stop some others from acquiring any one of the three types of WMD.

This may have the merit of intellectual honesty, but in turn is it sustainable politically? How can it be introduced or imposed as a WMD management regime? How will compliance be enforced?

This is where the blatant rejections of multilateral regimes by Washington have been so damaging to its own long-term interests. If the United States works hard at the message that it believes in multilateralism, including the pursuit of national interests through multilateral regimes, then more friends and allies may work to mute the rising tide of hostility towards US exceptionalism, which rests upon its conception of itself as a virtuous power that should not be bound to rules that apply to everyone else.

10

Unilateralism is not the way

The Japan Times, 13 May 2002

As the sole remaining superpower, not only does the United States have no peer competitor, its dominance is unmatched across a whole range of issues and areas of activity in world affairs.

Nevertheless, the United States is not the only actor in world affairs. Many countries are America's traditional friends and allies of long-standing. The gap between their total capacity and the military, economic, diplomatic and information technology assets that can be deployed by Washington on any issue, in any theatre of the world, has grown alarmingly wide over the course of the past decade. US dependence on allies has diminished from the Persian Gulf to the Kosovo and Afghanistan wars.

US interest in, and commitment to, multilateral regimes has waned in parallel to its accelerating dominance of the world stage. Paradoxically, the interests of its allies and friends have veered sharply towards multilateralism.

The Kyoto Protocol bears the footprints of Japan with regard to global warming; the Ottawa Treaty was signed against the backdrop of niche Canadian middle-power diplomacy; the Comprehensive Test Ban Treaty (CTBT) was saved from its near-death experience in Geneva by Australia and taken to the United Nations in New York for an emergency, life-saving operation.

Most recently, it was the like-minded allies and friends who led the campaign for the establishment of the International Criminal Court, which will come into operation later this year.

In unceremoniously rejecting all these painstakingly negotiated multi-lateral regimes, Washington is short-sightedly dismissive of its partners' national interests, which are embedded in multilateralism. Like all countries, they too would like to be thought of as virtuous. But their security policy rests on hard-nosed calculations of national interests, not on the pedestal of moral virtue.

Allies like Australia, Canada and Japan construct their national security architecture on four pillars: modern defence forces nationally; a robust military alliance with the United States that is continually reinterpreted and reinvigorated to realign it with the changing international strategic environment bilaterally; active defence-cooperation arrangements with compatible partners regionally; and multilateral arms control and other security regimes internationally.

Their pursuit of multilateral arms control is based on a careful judgment that such regimes contribute to their national security. Precisely because multilateral agreements are negotiated outcomes, they are typically imperfect bargains, reflecting the compromises that all sides had to make in the interests of getting an agreement that meets the minimum concerns of all parties while falling short of their maximum ambitions.

Japan was the midwife to the Kyoto Protocol – despite the small but continuing level of scientific uncertainty about global warming – because of the precautionary principle. This is the environmental analogue of the common safety rule for driving: if in doubt, don't.

Australia helped to broker the CTBT in the belief that technical improvements through continued nuclear testing were subordinate to the risks of nuclear proliferation if testing was not terminated.

Canada was the catalyst for the ban on antipersonnel landmines because their marginal military utility is outweighed by their anti-humanitarian carnage.

The Bush administration has discarded the Kyoto Protocol, rejected the CTBT and, if it implements parts of the recently leaked Nuclear Posture Review, will risk the unravelling of the Nuclear Non-Proliferation Treaty (NPT) – the most widely subscribed to arms control regime in history. US rejection of the CTBT is especially egregious for, as India argued in opposing it back in 1996, it actually locks in US margins of superiority against all other countries.

While the CTBT and NPT, along with the chemical and biological weapons conventions, the Ottawa Treaty and other international instruments, raise the threshold of proliferation and use, they simultaneously lower the bar to collective international responses for ensuring regime compliance. They thus lower the threat, reduce the need for counter-proliferation preparation and strategies, and promote norms of acceptable international behaviour.

In signing international arms control treaties, states accept binding obligations. If North Korea should seek to acquire nuclear weapons, NPT obligations give us significant leverage first to hold it to a legal contract, and second, if that is ignored, to fashion a collective response to non-compliance. It is far easier to form coalitions of the willing from those angered by non-compliance with international treaties and global norms – which is a good working definition of a rogue state.

Some fascinating recent research suggests that people will accept individual costs in order to collectively punish transgressors of key social norms. The same applies, I believe, to countries, for we all have a strongly developed sense of right and wrong.

Of course, no arms control regime can provide foolproof assurance against cheating. But the key issue, as in all aspects of life, is risk management. We don't stop driving or flying because of the risks of accidents. Rather, we take reasonable precautions, institute safety procedures, ensure minimum skills through approved testing procedures and set in place mechanisms and people for catching and punishing the violators of the collective norms of driving and flying.

There is no country on Earth in which people do not violate traffic laws and seek to evade detection. Some even succeed. It would be as irresponsible as it would be irrational to conclude that driving licence requirements and traffic codes should therefore be thrown out in favour of a free-for-all on the nation's roads.

So, yes, some states and groups will surely try to cheat on their international obligations. But the verification and monitoring mechanisms built into arms control regimes gives us a higher chance of catching them in efforts to cheat. The risk of detection acts as a deterrent against cheating, and the risk of being branded a cheat adds an element of compliance.

The United States can leverage its hard and soft power assets – its military might, economic muscle, diplomatic clout, voting weight in international financial institutions, etc. – to hold signatories to their international treaty obligations. If these are violated, the United States can leverage the same set of assets to forge coalitions of the willing, as in the Persian Gulf, Kosovo and Afghanistan wars over the past decade. The world needs American muscle and leadership on the side of the law-abiding.

The security guarantees of the North Atlantic Treaty Organization (NATO) across the Atlantic and the Australia, New Zealand and United States of America (ANZUS) security treaty across the Pacific were invoked, both for the first time ever, in the war on terror, to help the United States. Washington could reciprocate by underwriting multilateral arms control regimes that are important pillars of the national security architectures of most of its key allies, even if they be less relevant to US security interests directly. Doing so may not serve narrowly defined US national interests, but it would surely be in the enlightened self-interest of the United States.

11

Let's get together against terrorism

The International Herald Tribune, 4 June 2002

As we contemplate the awful prospect of terrorists using weapons of mass destruction, it is worth examining the merits of setting up an international commission to propose practical solutions.

The mid-1990s was the zenith of arms control and disarmament. It proved a false dawn. Recent trends, fuelled in particular by fears of terrorism after the horrific attacks on the United States last September, point in the opposite direction – towards a new dark age for disarmament as weapons of mass destruction and the means to deliver them spread not just to more states but to terrorist groups and other so-called substate actors. To try to prevent this, it is time to establish an International Commission on Weapons of Mass Destruction. Its mandate should cover nuclear, biological and chemical weapons that the Nuclear Non-Proliferation Treaty and biological and chemical weapons conventions have targeted for total elimination.

The commission's mandate should include both nonproliferation and disarmament. One cannot be sacrificed for the other. It should also cover possible terrorist uses of such weapons and ways of countering such threats.

One approach would be to set the commission up as a special United Nations panel; the other would be to have an independent commission. Either way, it should develop new ideas and explore practical means for applying them.

It should examine how to achieve sustainable disarmament, where arms are reduced to the level necessary to assure the national security needs of today's peoples and states without threatening the security and development needs of other countries and future generations.

It should look closely at verification technologies to eliminate all weapons of mass destruction and prevent new ones from being developed.

The commission's report could serve both as a call to action and an authoritative instrument for governments and nongovernmental organizations in advocating greater progress on disarmament. It could propose new approaches on how to verify compliance with the Biological Weapons Convention, expedite the entry into force of the Comprehensive Test Ban Treaty, and provide a roadmap for dealing with terrorist use of weapons of mass destruction without succumbing to overreaction or panic.

Having two co-chairs, one each from the North and the South, would be a political asset in harnessing legitimacy in both camps. The commission must comprise world-renowned and respected experts. It should be backed by an efficient secretariat, a politically attuned advisory board, the capacity to undertake in-depth research, and adequate funding. Follow-through will be vital.

International commissions need not be culs-de-sac. They can lead to breakthroughs in conceptual thinking with practical policy implications – like the Brundtland Commission's proposal for sustainable development, or the International Commission on Intervention and State Sovereignty with its innovative concept of the responsibility to protect.

Such advances are urgently needed to head off the spread of weapons of mass destruction.

Note

Article co-authored by Jayantha Dhanapala and Ramesh Thakur. At the time of the article's publication, Mr. Dhanapala was the United Nations under-secretary-general for disarmament. An international commission on weapons of mass destruction was subsequently set up by the Swedish government and published its report in late 2005. Chaired by Hans Blix, it included Mr. Dhanapala as a member.

12

Peacekeeping – Diplomacy's odd couple, the US and the UN

The International Herald Tribune, 26 June 2002

As the United Nations marks the 57th anniversary this Wednesday of the signing of its founding charter, many Americans see the United Nations as a pretentious, ponderous and pompous non-power in world affairs. They believe it should scale down its ambitions to a much more modest level.

The United States, of course, has much to be immodest about. The basic structure of the United Nations reflects the assumption of a world of five major powers. But today there is only one superpower, the United States, coexisting uneasily alongside only one overarching international organization.

Americans bemoan the inability of the United Nations to bring rogue states to heel. Yet many non-American critics of the United Nations also despair at the periodic US tendency to behave like a rogue superpower, responsible to no one but the US Congress and the American voter.

The terrorist attacks on America in September showed that the US homeland is vulnerable to quarrels rooted in complex conflicts in distant lands. Outsiders hoped that 9/11 would change the United States and prompt it to re-engage with the international community.

Yet it appears Americans concluded that 9/11 reduced their need to make concessions to the nebulous "international community" on vital national security issues.

But US power, wealth and politics are too deeply intertwined with the cross currents of international affairs for unilateral disengagement to be an option. The UN Security Council, the proper body for authorizing international use of military force, is bad at waging wars. As a result, maintaining world order in the past 50 years has depended more on US than UN ability and will.

The United States is uniquely qualified to be the sole superpower because it is a virtuous power. No other country, historically or in recent memory, has a better record of major power behaviour.

But Washington cannot construct a world in which all others have to obey universal norms and rules, while it can opt out on such norms concerning nuclear tests, landmines, international criminal prosecution, climate change and other regimes.

Peacekeeping will remain the instrument of choice for contemporary conflicts in places like Afghanistan, East Timor, Sierra Leone and the Balkans. Peacekeeping will thus define the United States-United Nations relationship.

If Washington is perceived to be unwilling to support peacekeeping in messy conflicts in faraway countries, it will erode America's ability to harness UN legitimacy to causes and battles that may be more important to the United States, such as the war on terrorism.

In addition to being the pivotal permanent member of the Security Council, the United States is the main financial underwriter of UN peace operations. It has unmatched influence on their establishment, mandate, nature, size and termination.

America's goal is to make UN peace operations efficient, cost effective and selective, increasing the professional military capabilities of the United Nations but leaving war fighting to multinational coalitions.

The level of informed American interest about the United Nations is so low that any administration will always be able to distance itself from spectacular failures of UN peacekeeping, as with Somalia and Srebrenica. Washington was jointly culpable in both disasters.

US participation in enforcement operations under direct UN command can be ruled out. Its participation in other operations, whose creation requires US consent, will be limited to providing key transport, communications and logistics units and skills, and bearing the main financial burden.

UN peace operations – some of which are coalitions of the unwilling, unable and unlike minded – are only one of many foreign policy tools available to the United States. Others include multilateral action through the North Atlantic Treaty Organization (Kosovo), ad hoc multinational coalitions (the Gulf War), or unilateral action if vital US interests are involved.

In non-UN operations, the United States would prefer to act after Security Council authorization, but will not accept that as a mandatory requirement for the use of military force overseas. The United States has an equally compelling interest in promoting the norm that the United Nations is the only acceptable legitimator of international military action for all except the United States and NATO.

Washington thus faces a tough dilemma between instilling the principle of multilateralism as the norm of world order, and exempting itself from the same principle because of a strong belief in exceptionalism – and in its identity as the virtuous power.

13

Politics vs. justice at The Hague: The International Criminal Court

The International Herald Tribune, 16 August 2002

The policy of the United States towards the International Criminal Court (ICC) appears to put politics over justice. But it has more merit than critics allow.

The US position ensures that Americans continue to have full safeguards as criminal defendants. It is also consistent with balancing the competing requirements of peace, justice and reconciliation.

The ICC is not embedded in a broader system of democratic policy making. There is no political check on it. In claiming jurisdiction over nationals of countries that are not members of the court, it displaces the state as the conduit of democratic representation without providing an alternative. Why should it have authority over a constitutionally legitimated democracy like the United States?

Washington may have been tripped by its own moves in setting up the international criminal tribunals for Yugoslavia and Rwanda, which generated an unstoppable momentum for a permanent court with universal jurisdiction. Yet the Hague and Arusha tribunals began as substitutes for effective action to halt preventable atrocities; they were not indicators of toughening new standards of international judicial accountability. By keeping them under the jurisdiction of the United Nations Security Council, the United States made sure that it controlled their destiny.

For justice to be done, it is important that the rule-of-law standard is scrupulously observed in the collection and presentation of evidence, the right to cross-examination of witnesses, and all other procedures that we associate with a fair trial. In the US legal culture in particular, human rights law gives primacy to protecting the rights of the arrested and the accused over the requirements of the prosecution for securing conviction.

Impelled by the momentum of international accountability, the balance has shifted: the conviction rates of the ad hoc international tribunals have been notably higher than for criminal prosecutions in the United States. Washington itself has been complicit in this transformation from protecting the rights of the accused to privileging the case for the prosecution.

Criminal law, however effective, cannot replace public or foreign policy. Determining the fate of defeated leaders is primarily a political question, not a judicial one. The legal clarity of judicial verdicts sits uncomfortably with the nuanced morality of confronting and overcoming, through a principled mix of justice and high politics, a troubled past.

A criminal trial is not always the best instrument for collective memory and communal healing. It can cause more damage and solidify the very social cleavages that led to genocide and ethnic cleansing.

The international criminal justice route takes away from concerned societies the right to decide whether, how and who to prosecute for alleged mass crimes, and what punishment to inflict on those found guilty. It also takes away from them the options of alternative modes of reconciliation. The purely juridical approach to transitional justice traps and suspends communities in the prism of past hatreds.

South Africa, Mozambique and Rwanda have all made deliberate policy choices to escape cycles of retributive violence. The record of "restorative" justice systems in bringing closure to legacies of systematic savagery is superior to that of institutions of international criminal justice; the latter's closure is more authoritative but also more partial and premature.

Just as any law constrains any power, so international law would constrain US international power: There lies the rub. Washington bridles at the audacity of the "international community" in wanting to constrain US international behaviour. For Washington, the United Nations exists to expand national policy options, not limit them.

But the US rejection of the ICC betrays a curious mixture of exceptionalism – the self-image of a good and great people divinely ordained to lead the world by example at home and activism abroad – and power politics: Why concede equal status to inferiors?

The ICC's attraction is its global scope, giving it the authority to investigate heinous international crimes wherever, whenever and by whoever they are committed. Only universal liability can arrest and reverse the drift to ad hoc universalism, from Nuremberg and Tokyo to the Yugoslavia and Rwanda tribunals.

14

Peril of preemptive thinking

The Japan Times, 20 October 2002

Should Washington go to war unilaterally, it will put at risk the hard-earned reputation since 1945 of being an essentially peaceful hegemon that fights only in self-defence – unlike the former Soviet Union, the expansionist bully that dressed up its aggression in the rhetoric of a universal socialist brotherhood. And what if the United Nations Security Council authorizes war? When the infamous resolution equating Zionism with racism was adopted, it was less a triumph of Arab diplomacy than an indictment of UN pusillanimity. If the United Nations should be seen to have bent to US will, who will protect UN officials against retaliatory attacks?

Since much of the US grievance against Iraq seems to be focused on Iraqi President Saddam Hussein's nuclear weapons program – and the American anger has precipitated an international crisis through the threat of war – it is worth examining the impact of 9/11 on nuclear weapons and doctrines and world order.

If by the end of his term, US President Bill Clinton was a reluctant multilateralist, at the start of his term President George W. Bush was a disengaged multilateralist. The terrorist attacks of 11 September 2001 pushed him into an assertive and aggressive unilateralism with little inclination to make concessions on any front to international concerns.

The dismissive attitude towards global regimes has found expression in unilateral changes in US doctrines with respect to the utility and usability of nuclear weapons. Mutual and extended deterrence (for allies sheltered under the nuclear umbrella) has given way to offensive deterrence and unilateral preemption with special-purpose nuclear weapons that have been transformed from weapons of last resort to weapons of choice. There is further mission creep. Where previously their use was unimaginable except against nuclear enemies, today they are justified as counters to "weapons of mass destruction," including biological and chemical weapons.

But such doctrinal spread may have unhappy consequences for weapons proliferation. For the calculus of potential proliferators is bound to be changed in response to the changing US doctrine. Lowering the threshold of their use weakens the taboo against them, thus inevitably lowering the normative barriers to nuclear proliferation.

The proclamation of an essentially imperial doctrine of unchallenged military supremacy and full-spectrum dominance will greatly magnify the allure of nuclear weapons as weapons of defence and deterrence for poor/weak countries. Moreover, the combination of US high-tech superiority, reliance on long distance over-the-horizon warfare and casualty aversion adds value to nuclear weapons as leveraging tools that can affect the calculus of US military decisions.

But this in itself is now less worrying to Washington. For yet another effect of 9/11 was to change dramatically the focus of concern from universal to differentiated nuclear proliferation. Previously, the Nuclear Non-Proliferation Treaty (NPT) was the centrepiece and embodiment of the nonproliferation norm. This is why sanctions were imposed on India and Pakistan for carrying out nuclear tests in 1998, even though neither had signed the NPT.

Now the US concern is not in relation to the NPT, but in terms of the relations of the proliferators with Washington. US-friendly countries like Israel never evoked outrage over their nuclear weapons programs. Since 9/11, even India and Pakistan have been lifted out of countries of concern in favour of concentrated attacks on the axis of evil countries – that is, US-hostile proliferators.

And of course the concern is no longer limited to state proliferators, but extends much more broadly to nonstate groups and individuals as well, especially those who might some day contemplate acts of nuclear terrorism. This is the true meaning of the Bush promise that the United States will not allow the world's most dangerous weapons to fall into the hands of the world's most dangerous regimes (and, one might add, the world's most destructive groups and individuals), as judged solely and unilaterally by Washington.

Therein lies the logic of preemption, if necessary, well before the threat actually materializes (as with Hussein, whose acquisition of nuclear weapons does not seem imminent, all bluster to the contrary notwithstanding). There is also an underlying belief that current criticism of any US-led war to take out Hussein's weapons of mass destruction will be quickly muted with the success of the operation and eventually turn into gratitude for someone's having had the necessary foresight, fortitude and resolution.

But in turn this changes the basis of world order as we know it. And that might be the most profound and long-lasting significance of 9/11. It may indeed have changed the world and tipped us into a post-Westphalian world. US policy is full of contradictions within the paradigm of world order since the Treaty of Westphalia (1648) wherein all states are of equal status and legitimacy.

How can the most prominent dissident against many global norms and regimes – from arms control to climate change and international criminal justice – claim to be the world's most powerful enforcer of global norms and regimes, including nonproliferation?

How can the most vocal critic of the very notion of an international community anoint itself as the international community's sheriff? For that matter, by what right do the five unelected members of the Security Council claim a permanent monopoly on nuclear weapons?

The answer lies in a conception of world order rooted outside the framework of Westphalian sovereignty. This also explains why some of today's most potent threats come not from the conquering states within the Westphalian paradigm, but from failing states outside it.

In effect, Bush is saying that the gap between the fiction of legal equality and the reality of power preponderance, between equally legitimate and democratically legitimate states, has stretched beyond the breaking point.

Washington is no longer bound by such fiction. The Bush administration insists that the United States will remain as fundamentally trustworthy, balanced and responsible a custodian of world order as before – but of a post-Westphalian order centred on the United States surrounded by a wasteland of vassal states.

The United Nations is an organization of member states. During the mini-crisis in the Security Council in July over the International Criminal Court, Washington had already demonstrated that it views the United Nations as a forum for augmenting policy options – not limiting them.

In his address to the General Assembly last month, Bush modified the "if you are not with us, you are against us" slogan from the war on terror to "if you are not with us, you are irrelevant" for the coming war against Iraq. This was not an American concession to UN multilateralism, but a demand for international capitulation to the US threat to go to war. But in doing so, Bush presented the United Nations with an impossible choice between credibility and effectiveness, on the one hand, and integrity and principle, on the other.

The United Nations is both the symbol and the major instrument for moderating the use of force in international affairs, not sanctifying it and blessing a major expansion in its permissive scope through such subjective subterfuges as preemption. And it is the collective body for protecting the territorial integrity of member states within the Westphalian paradigm of national sovereignty.

The choice between irrelevance (for not having the courage to enforce its decisions) and complicity (in endorsing an armed attack on the territorial integrity of the weak by the powerful) would be a fatal one for the organization.

15

India and Israel: United in trauma of terror

The Japan Times, 19 December 2002

While India is the world's most populous democracy, Israel is the Middle East's most notable. Relations between democratic countries can be strained on particular issues, but the underlying strength remains resilient. Judaism and Hinduism are among the world's ancient civilizations and "root faiths" that have given birth to other major religions. They are similar in their emphasis on the practice of rituals as an integral element of their respective faiths, and the distinctive Jewish humour also resonates well in India. India's tradition of hospitality towards the Jewish people is centuries old. Even in the Hindu-Muslim butchery at the birth of independent India, Jews were not harmed.

India's relationship with Israel, which gained independence within a year of India's in a similarly traumatic partition, was a major anomaly. One of the earliest to recognize Israel, India was one of the last to establish full ambassadorial relations with it in 1992. Full relations were maintained with China and Pakistan, countries with which India has major territorial conflicts and has fought wars – but not with Israel, with whom India had no direct quarrel.

The policy of distance provoked Israeli resentment and US cynicism about India's moral authority, but without materially assisting the Palestinian cause or buying Arab goodwill when it mattered. India's first prime minister, Jawaharlal Nehru, conceded in 1958 that his Israel policy was not "a matter of high principle." It was based on pre-independence sympathy by the Congress Party for the Arabs, a perception of Israel as a settlement imposed on the Arabs by outgoing colonial powers, the higher number of Arab votes at the United Nations instead of the solitary Israeli vote, an attempt to avoid the full weight of Arab support going to Pakistan, and sensitivity to Indian Muslims, who make up 12 percent of the country's own population.

The non-policy on Israel sometimes degenerated into petty petulance: a refusal to permit the Indian tennis team to play a Davis Cup tie against Israel, or the refusal to permit an Indian film to be screened at an Israeli film festival or even let the film director attend the festival. In 1993, the Jerusalem Symphony Orchestra was scheduled to perform in Bombay and New Delhi. India, describing Jerusalem as a disputed city, insisted that the orchestra drop "Jerusalem" from its name; the orchestra dropped the India visit instead.

At other times, India's quixotic policy on Israel produced odd strategic choices. Much criticized at the time for taking out Iraq's nuclear reactor in 1981, Israel has been amply vindicated since. Apparently in the early 1980s, Israel thrice proposed to India that the two should jointly attack and destroy Pakistan's nuclear plant at Kahuta. The Israeli Air Force was confident of achieving the pinpoint accuracy needed to destroy the facility, but needed refuelling facilities in western India because of the distances involved.

Like Shakespeare's Caesar with the kingly crown, India thrice refused: Enmity should be made of sterner stuff. Israel concluded that India's hesitation stemmed from Soviet pressure and an unwillingness to compromise its paper status as a nonaligned leader. Thus India has shown neither the political courage to address and resolve the Kashmir problem through bilateral dialogue with Pakistan, nor the courage of its convictions in viewing its neighbour as an enemy.

In a book published in 1994 (*The Politics and Economics of India's Foreign Policy*), having described India's Israel policy as neither principled nor pragmatic, I argued that they had many common interests: "India could also learn much from Israel and the United States on how to combat the scourge of domestic and international terrorism."

How things have changed! India and Israel discovered common concerns in the growth of Islamic fundamentalism in Central and Southwest Asia, and by the end of the 20th century they were truly united in the trauma of terrorism as an everyday reality. High-level and well-publicized delegations now exchange visits all the time; security cooperation seems to be deepening and broadening; bilateral trade is thriving (albeit from a low base); Israel is India's second-best military supplier after Russia; and within the foreseeable future, India could become Israel's best market for military sales.

In an article in the *New Republic* in February this year, Yossi Klein Halevi argued that as well as shared interests and fears India and Israel have discovered a common purpose, and young Israelis have fallen under the spell of the romance of India. Over the past decade over a quarter-million Israelis, mostly young people, have visited India.

Ironically, the immediate aftermath of 9/11 last year drove India and Israel closer together almost in common resentment of US courtship of Islamic countries that were countries of concern in their history of harbouring cross-border terrorism. They shared the sense that 9/11 was probably a one-off attack on the United States, whereas for them cross-border terrorism is a life and death struggle in the immediate vicinity. Of course, critics of India and Israel would argue that the policies of both countries contribute to the growth and sustenance of militant resistance against them.

India's quest for intimate relations with the United States is helped by close relations with Israel. Good relations between the United States, the European Union, Israel, India and Japan, linked appropriately to southern hemisphere democracies but not directed against any specific countries or groups, would form a powerful and influential arc of democracies encircling the globe. It might also make for an effective firewall against global terrorism.

16

US test of UN relevance

The Japan Times, 9 February 2003

Time was when those threatening to go to war had to prove their case beyond reasonable doubt. Today we are asked to prove to the powerful, to their satisfaction, why they should not go to war. The UN inspectors don't have to prove that Iraq has weapons of mass destruction; Iraqi President Saddam Hussein has to prove that he doesn't. The gap between world public opinion that has hardened against a war and the voting equation in the Security Council in New York presents a rare opportunity for diluting the cynicism of Soviet-era dissident Alexander Solzhenitsyn's remark that, at the United Nations, the people of the world are served up to the designs of governments.

There is a sense of helpless anger about hurtling towards a war no one wants. In Canada, Europe and Asia, the depth of alienation from US policy on Iraq is quite striking. In India, people dub it "dadagiri": bullying by the neighbourhood tough in a global neighbourhood.

West Europeans use startlingly strong language for the Bush administration's "monomaniacal focus on Iraq." Because of US ability to twist governments' arms in bilateral dealings, the gap between popular opinion and government policy is often very wide, and the resulting anger and bitterness for this too is directed at Washington.

After 9/11, US President George W. Bush famously asked: Why do they hate America? A multinational survey conducted late last year by the US-based Pew Research Center documented a rising tide of hostility to US foreign policy alongside a continuing affirmation of bedrock American values. A poll last month showed that more than one-third of

Canadians believe the Bush administration to be the most dangerous for world peace, far more than the number holding such a view of Hussein. *New York Times* columnist Nicholas Kristof notes that on 9/11, "they" meant the Arabs; today it means everybody.

There are many Iraq-centred reasons for the precipitously declining confidence in US leadership.

Few outsiders are convinced of the case for war. Little evidence links Hussein to al-Qaeda leader Osama bin Laden. Hussein has been successfully contained and does not pose a clear and present danger to regional, world or US security. Washington has scarcely concealed its real agenda of regime change, which is why the UN inspection process is seen as an instrument of mass distraction.

There is confusion about the mix of personal, oil, geopolitical and military-technological motives for going to war. Two things are widely believed to follow from the contrasting US policies towards Iraq and North Korea: Iraq does not have usable nuclear weapons, North Korea does not have oil.

Bush's address to the General Assembly in September was interpreted less as a US concession to UN multilateralism than a demand for international capitulation to Washington. Many governments are seen as pursuing a policy of appeasement of the United States as today's dominant power determined to get its way by the threat of war. Imagine if in 1938, in trying to avert war, the League of Nations had added its weight to Franco-British pressure on Czechoslovakia to cede the Sudetenland to Hitler and had endorsed the Munich Pact: would this have made the League "relevant" to the needs and events of its day?

Hussein's is an odious regime that has grievously wronged its own people, neighbours and the international community. But, as Joost Hiltermann noted in *The New York Times*, cynicism about US motives runs deep because of its history of past material and diplomatic support for Hussein during the days when his behaviour was at its worst, including the use of chemical weapons against his own people in Halabja and the attack on Iran.

Then there is cynicism over the five permanent members of the UN Security Council – the five nuclear powers – demanding immediate non-proliferation from everyone else while permanently deferring their own nuclear disarmament. In recent years, the United States has belittled and hollowed out a series of arms control and disarmament agreements and thwarted efforts at ushering in new ones. Nuclear weapons are seemingly advancing up the ladder of escalation from the weapon of last resort, matching the shift from wars of self-defence to wars of choice.

Washington underestimates how its rhetoric and actions worsen the proliferation challenge. The world has signed on to the Nuclear Non-

Proliferation Treaty (NPT); Washington exempts itself from NPT clauses requiring nuclear disarmament. Small states put their faith in the protection of international law; Washington is disdainfully dismissive: international law will follow not shape the sole superpower's behaviour. Small states pin their hopes for security from predatory powers on a functioning UN system; the United States declares the United Nations to be irrelevant unless supportive of what Washington desires, even while demanding Iraqi compliance with UN resolutions, and issues threats of unilateral preemptive strikes.

The proclamation of an imperial doctrine of unchallengeable military dominance magnifies the allure of nuclear weapons for poor and weak countries. As Washington throws off its fetters on the unilateral use of force and the universal taboo on nuclear weapons, it simultaneously increases the attraction of nuclear weapons for others – like North Korea – and diminishes the force of global norms and regimes in restraining their nuclear ambitions.

Voices have been raised even in allied countries that a war should not be supported even if authorized by the United Nations. In Australia about 20 Labor lawmakers are reportedly opposed to war even if it is UN-sanctioned. The New Democratic Party in Canada has pondered a similar line. *The Australian* columnist Philip Adams argues that the Bush regime "has bullied and browbeaten the United Nations into submission."

In Britain, Seamus Milne wrote that "even if the United States is able to bribe and bully its way to a new UN resolution in the face of world opinion," the "endorsement will lack any genuine international legitimacy" as "a multiple violation of the UN Charter." And Madeleine Bunting writes of "UN window-dressing to decorate American belligerence with international legitimacy." Not so long ago, former South African President Nelson Mandela was hailed by London and Washington as the conscience of Africa. On 30 January he was quoted as criticizing the US stance on Iraq as "arrogant," aimed at gaining control of Iraqi oil, and likely to cause a "holocaust." He described Tony Blair as acting more like the "US foreign minister."

These are deeply worrying portents for the United Nations. Fortunately they represent, at least for now, a minority strand of opinion. The clear majority wants the UN stamp of legitimacy as a precondition for war. But if it simply confers a blank cheque then, instead of UN legitimacy being stamped on military action against Iraq, the legitimacy of the United Nations itself will be eroded. Already, in a 39-nation Gallup poll conducted in January, a majority (50–60 percent) of Germans, French, Indians and Russians oppose a war on Iraq even with UN authorization; in Britain, 41 percent are opposed to war under any circumstance, while 39 percent support UN-sanctioned action. In most countries, the cover of UN sanction is enough to tip the scales for majority support.

There will indeed be occasions and opponents where UN diplomacy must be backed by US force. But a "wrong war" will damage the instrument and delegitimize the institution. Washington may be irritated at the delays, but treading the UN path has helped to correct the balance between "We the peoples" and "You the governments" of the world. That is the true test of UN relevance: both as a brake on an unjustified or unilateral resort to war, and as the forum of choice for legitimizing the military enforcement of international community demands on outlaw regimes.

17

US bears costs as UN is challenged

The Japan Times, 12 March 2003

As the issue of Iraq comes to a head, the United Nations faces a grave challenge. The five permanent members of the UN Security Council are deeply divided; many governments – British, Japanese, Spanish, Turkish – are at odds with their own people; and the divisions have hardened since US President George W. Bush made his dramatic address to the General Assembly in September. Three different perspectives exist on the challenge posed to the United Nations:

* The first perspective is the US warning of irrelevance if the United Nations fails to enforce its resolutions on recalcitrant outlaws. The terrorist attacks of 11 September 2001 removed the cobwebs from the strategic big picture. For Washington the issues could hardly be more serious. Iraq is ruled by a "rogue regime" that has vigorously pursued the clandestine acquisition of weapons of mass destruction; used biochemical weapons against its own citizens and neighbouring Iran; engaged in some of the most horrific human rights atrocities; attacked Iran and invaded and annexed Kuwait; and defied the United Nations for 12 long years.

Can one of the world's most dangerous regimes be permitted to remain in power until it succeeds in acquiring the world's most dangerous weapons? The concurrent crisis with North Korea proves the wisdom of dealing with Iraqi President Saddam Hussein now, before he gains his hands on nuclear or other equally powerful weapons – for it will be next to impossible to defang him after he has usable weapons of mass destruction and delivery systems. The typically foggy lens of multilateralism has been confronted by the moral clarity claimed by an administration that, distinguishing good from evil, is determined to promote one and destroy the other.

Meanwhile, America's threat of war has galvanized the United Nations into putting teeth into the inspection machinery and produced unprecedented cooperation from the Iraqis. If there is a swift and decisive war; if the ouster of Hussein paves the way for a brighter and happier future for Iraqis and lets a hundred flowers of freedom bloom in the arid Arab desert; and if this is done without UN authorization, then the credibility and authority of the United Nations will be gravely damaged, and the prestige and mana of the United States greatly enhanced.

Conversely, under this first perspective, it is assumed that cooperation from Baghdad will not last forever. As international pressure slackens, Hussein will return to his familiar game of cheat and retreat. His survival following full US military mobilization will gravely dent US global credibility. Should that happen, the United Nations, which has no independent military capability, will lose its most potent enforcement agent even as other would-be tyrants are emboldened. The resulting political backlash in the United States could well imperil continued American membership, and the United Nations could become this century's League of Nations.

* The second point of view acknowledges the need to confront Hussein, but rules out acting without UN authorization. The Security Council lies at the centre of the international law enforcement system. It is the chief body for building, consolidating and using the authority of the international community. The challenge is not to find alternatives to it, but to make it work better. Bypassing it will undermine it and put at risk the very foundations of a secure and just world order. The United Nations is our only hope for unity in diversity in a world where global problems require multilateral solutions.

UN legitimacy has been steadily eroding because of perceptions of the Security Council's unrepresentative composition, undemocratic operation, lack of accountability to anyone "below" like the General Assembly or "above" like the World Court, plus ineffectiveness. Americans often mock the last failing. But if it were to become increasingly activist, interventionist and effective, then the lack of representational and procedural legitimacy and judicial accountability would lead many others to resist the authority of the Security Council even more forcefully.

* The third argument accepts UN authorization as necessary, but not sufficient. There is growing disquiet that the United Nations is being subverted to the US agenda for war. It risks becoming to the United States what the Warsaw Pact was to the old Soviet Union: a collective mechanism for legitimizing the dominant power's hegemonism. It cannot be the case that the United Nations is harnessed to US interests when convenient but trashed otherwise.

UN credibility could be in tatters if Iraq is attacked by the United States with its ability for self-defence sharply degraded after months of disarmament by the United Nations. As chief weapons inspector Hans Blix put it, the Iraqis have not been breaking toothpicks when they destroy their missiles.

Reasons for the strong worldwide anti-war sentiment include doubts about the justification for going to war; anxiety over the human toll, uncontrollable course and incalculable consequences of a war in an already inflamed region; and scepticism that the United States will stay engaged – politically, economically and militarily – for the years of reconstruction required after a war.

Washington is seen as determined to wage war not because it has to, but because it wants to and can. Hussein was on this administration's agenda when it came into office. The 9/11 attacks provided the excuse, not the reason. Advances in military technology make it possible to complete the unfinished agenda from the 1990–91 Persian Gulf War. Washington has found it especially difficult to convince others of the need to go to war now, and has not helped its cause by a continually shifting justification.

Containment and deterrence worked against the far more formidable Soviet enemy during the Cold War. Why should they be replaced by the destabilizing doctrine of preemption? Excessive comments and opinion about the post-war scenario have strengthened suspicions of a predetermined agenda for war.

The United Nations has not escaped this dilemma. If it does not prepare in advance for a post-war humanitarian challenge, it will be accused of criminal neglect of a predictable contingency. But if it does prepare for the contingency, it is accused of implicitly accepting an assault on the fundamental principles of the UN Charter instead of actively fighting such a gross violation of international norms prohibiting the use and threat of force.

In 1990, in flagrant violation of the UN Charter, Iraq invaded Kuwait; the United Nations strongly supported a war to eject the Iraqis. In 2001 the United States was attacked by terrorists; the United Nations rallied to the American call for waging war on the terrorists and on Afghanistan's Taliban government that had given them a territorial base. This time, the crisis is seen to be the result of US belligerence, not Iraqi aggression. If the Security Council does authorize war, it will be seen as caving in to American threats and thus lacking the courage of UN convictions.

People look to the United Nations to stop war, not wage one. The United Nations is the chief symbol and instrument for moderating the use of force in international relations.

Some in civil society say the crisis has heightened the need for a global peoples' assembly to counter the repeated betrayals by an intergovernmental organization. Others look to the UN secretary-general as the last line of defence of the UN Charter principles. But this places an impossible burden on the world's top international civil servant. If the Security Council is united, the secretary-general cannot be an alternative voice of dissent; if it is divided, he cannot be a substitute for inaction.

The costs already incurred before a war has begun include fissures in the three great institutions of peace and order since World War II: the United Nations, the North Atlantic Treaty Organization and the European Union. Al-Qaeda leader Osama bin Laden is still at large and regaining popularity among Muslims. While markets keep falling, hostility to US policy is on the rise. So is the price of oil.

North Korea has taken advantage of the US preoccupation with Iraq to throw off international fetters and restart its nuclear weapons program. And in the United States itself, civil liberties are being compromised on a scale not seen since McCarthyism in the 1950s.

With successes like these, why should America's enemies pray for US failure? Their joy and delight is the despair and distress of well-wishers and admirers of much that is so great and inspirational about America.

18

The United Nations: More relevant now than ever

The Japan Times, 23 March 2003

A Tale of Two Cities by Charles Dickens, set in revolutionary France, begins with the observation that it was the best of times and the worst of times. So might it be said, thanks in no small measure to France, of the tale of two cities of contemporary times, namely Washington and New York, the political capitals of the United States and the world, respectively.

It was not supposed to be so.

Back in September, having apparently decided to make war on Iraq to force out Iraqi President Saddam Hussein, dead or alive, Washington sought the United Nations' blessing for its military action. The message was clear and blunt: we will wage war, with or without your approval; if you are not with us, you will become irrelevant.

Then a funny thing happened on the road to Baghdad. The people of the world defected from the United States and converted to the United Nations. Instead of being a pro forma test of UN relevance, the agenda shifted to become a litmus test of US legitimacy. The issue transcends the insignificance of Hussein. It has morphed into the question of what sort of world we wish to live in.

The United Nations has been front and centre in the debate, the focus of hopes, fears and the media's most pressing attention. The United States signalled that it would play by the rules of the world body it helped create if, and only if, that institution bent to America's will. This, coming after years of US exceptionalism, united the rest of the world against US unilateralism. The more the Americans protested about UN irrelevance, the more the rest stubbornly dug in their heels to demonstrate its increasing relevance.

The Bush administration and the increasingly isolated government of British Prime Minister Tony Blair went to great lengths to cajole, bribe and coerce the six "swing votes" on the UN Security Council to support the war option. They would not have done so, though, if they had truly believed the United Nations to be irrelevant. Deeply convinced of the moral righteousness of their cause, Bush and Blair craved the United Nations' imprimatur to give their war the stamp of political and legal · authority.

Their determined rush to war ignited a worldwide debate on the legitimacy of war, the likes of which we have not seen before. The Security Council played precisely the role envisaged for it by the founders of the United Nations; it did so for six long months. It was more of a central player in this crisis than at any other time in its history.

From being an optional add-on in September, the Security Council became the forum of choice for making the case for the use of military force – for debating openly, publicly and globally the merits, wisdom, legality and legitimacy of war. This was a critical and historic dialogue that the world had to have, and we owe a deep debt of thanks to the Bush administration for it.

A globalized public opinion mobilized in opposition to the war before it even began. That global public opinion is broadly opposed to any war with Iraq that is not authorized by the Council. Moreover, for all the hard-nosed indifference to the United Nations feigned by tough-minded journalists, the crisis also brought the Council's deliberations unparalleled attention around the world. The United Nations as a global forum provided a platform for voicing domestic dissent within the United States. For the first time ever in human history, the international community united to wage peace before a war started. Call it the people's preemption.

Except in cases of self-defence, only the UN Security Council can decide whether it is lawful to go to war – not the United States, not Britain, not any other state.

As the influential *New York Times* columnist Thomas Friedman has noted, if Iraq was a war of necessity (self-defence), the United States could go it alone. But because it is a war of choice (regime change, which Friedman supports for humanitarian and democratic reasons), it needs the United Nations' blessing. UN Secretary-General Kofi Annan commands no more divisions and tanks than the pope. But both command enormous respect and authority. Annan's recent statement in a press conference at The Hague – that war without UN authorization would be outside the Charter and therefore implicitly illegal – has attracted great attention.

His presence at The Hague was a reminder too that the United Nations remains engaged on a wide range of fronts around the world, from reducing poverty and promoting good governance and universal literacy to protecting the environment, combating disease, undertaking peace operations and creating a permanent international criminal court. These issues, and the United Nations' engagement with them, will remain long after the Iraq crisis blows over.

Despite its manifest failings, the United Nations remains an extraordinarily resilient institution. Those who argue that the current war, waged without UN authorization, has rendered the United Nations irrelevant are either disingenuous or have very short memories. During the Cold War, superpower rivalry prevented the United Nations from playing any effective global security role. Only in rare cases, like the Korean War – when the Russians were foolishly boycotting the Council – was it possible for the use of force to receive UN authorization. Yet the United Nations survived this sorry period, as well as the disasters of Srebrenica, Somalia and – worst of all – Rwanda (which was more a failure of nerve and civic courage on the part of the United States than the United Nations). It will survive the current crisis as well.

After the war ends, the United Nations will again be called on to play a crucial role. This is precisely what happened in Kosovo when a "coalition of the willing" last went to war without UN authority. America and its allies fought the war; the United Nations led the arduous but critical task of post-conflict reconstruction. Far from being "irrelevant," the United Nations' role will be just as pivotal in the Iraqi case.

What of the veto? Many argue that it is an outmoded relic of the Cold War. They have a point. But the United States is in no position to criticize others. France has exercised its veto relatively rarely and usually only in concert with its allies. Russia, which had the dubious distinction of casting most vetoes during the Cold War, has been similarly restrained over the past decade. Since the end of the Cold War it is the United States that has wielded the veto most frequently – and almost always to block broadly supported resolutions critical of Israeli policies towards the Palestinians.

In the end the International Commission on Intervention and State Sovereignty (ICISS) came down unmistakably on the side of the central role of the United Nations as the indispensable font of international authority and the irreplaceable forum for authorizing international military enforcement.

The people of the world, having examined the US case for war against

Iraq, have put their faith in the United Nations and vindicated the ICISS conclusions.

The claim that the United Nations has become "irrelevant" by refusing to go along with a war to depose Hussein should be seen for what it is – patently false and wholly self-serving. Irrelevant? They should be so lucky. What began as a dispiriting challenge to all of us who believe in the irreducible symbolism and ideal of the United Nations has turned into an exhilarating affirmation of the centrality and relevance of the world body.

Note

Article co-authored by Andrew Mack and Ramesh Thakur. From 1998 to 2001, Mr. Mack was the director of the Strategic Planning Unit in the Executive Office of UN Secretary-General Kofi Annan. He now serves as the director of the Human Security Center at the Liu Institute for Global Issues at the University of British Columbia. Mr. Thakur, vice-rector of the United Nations University in Tokyo, was an ICISS commissioner.

19

War vindicates UN stance

The Japan Times, 27 April 2003

Are not the scenes of joy and jubilation from Iraq an embarrassing indictment of the United Nations' failure to support the war? Well, no,
not really. On the contrary, the course and outcome of the war is a strong
vindication of the UN stance. The big story of this war so far surely has
been proof that the United Nations was right, that Iraqi President Saddam Hussein did not possess usable weapons of mass destruction, and
therefore he did not pose a threat to regional, US or world security of
an urgency and gravity that required instant war to topple him. The UN
inspectors could indeed have been given more time to complete their job.
After all, they destroyed more Iraqi armaments between 1991 and 1998
than did the multinational coalition during the 1991 Persian Gulf War
itself.

Moreover, the speed of the victory by the American, British and Australian forces (the three countries that made up the coalition of the willing on this occasion) vindicates those opponents of the war who argued
that Hussein had been so weakened since 1991 that he did not pose a
credible threat to anyone outside Iraq. To credit the lightning victory to
brilliant coalition generalship rather than basic Iraqi weakness is a triumph of spin over substance.

Hussein did of course pose a grave threat to the human security of his
own people within Iraq's borders. But that was not the stated justification
for trying to get the UN Security Council to authorize military action. So
the euphoria following his defeat does not damn the United Nations' fail-

ure to authorize war – unless of course the coalition governments are prepared to argue that their real goal all along was regime change. But that would mean that for six months since September they engaged in an elaborate charade at the United Nations in claiming that the issue was an imminent and serious threat posed by Hussein's weapons of mass destruction.

The ouster of Hussein flows from strategic not ethical calculations of foreign policy. It is difficult to be joyous at the descent from the ideal of a world based on the rule of law to that of the law of the jungle – though one can see why the lion would welcome such a change.

If I have witnessed murder and know who the murderer is, but that person escapes justice through the clever pyrotechnics of an expensive trial lawyer, do I have the right to take the law into my own hands and kill him? And does the cheering by the victim's family vindicate my vigilante justice? For that is what regime change in Iraq amounts to.

How many are ready to accept the doctrine that the administration of the day in Washington may decide who is to be which country's leader, and who is to be toppled? Perhaps some kind reader will enlighten me about the last occasion when, faced with a choice between a pro-US strongman and a democratic resistance movement, Washington actually sided with the people against the tyrant. Or the last time that Washington urged the abolition of the veto power of the five permanent members because it was an obstacle to effective decision-making by the United Nations.

This is not to deny that many of today's institutions and systems are indeed out of date and incapable of meeting contemporary challenges. The basis of world order, with the United Nations at the centre of the system of global governance, has come under increasing strain in recent years.

One reason for this is the growing disconnect between the threats to peace and security, and the obstacles to economic development, lying increasingly within rather than between states. A second reason is the growing gravity of threats rooted in nonstate actors, including but not limited to terrorists. A third is the growing salience of weapons of mass destruction that in their reach and destructiveness challenge the basis of the territorial state. And the fourth is the growing disparity between the power of the United States and that of all others, and the challenge that this poses to the Westphalian fiction of sovereign states equal in status and legitimacy.

In short, the evolution of institutions of international governance has lagged behind the rapid emergence of collective problems with on-border and cross-border dimensions. The solution to this lies in amending existing rules and institutions. If they are incapable of change, they deserve to be abandoned, but only when replaced by new and improved successor laws and institutions. Otherwise, in the resulting authority vacuum, anarchy rules – and this is not okay.

. I would be delighted if we insist that only governments that are democratic at the national level can take part in democratic decision-making at the international level – but first let us embed that principle in international institutions.

"Regime change" lies at the intersection of two major trends under UN auspices. The first is the progressive universalization of the human rights norm carried out through a large number of legal conventions and promoted, however imperfectly, through a substantial legal machinery. The second is the central and irreplaceable role of the Security Council as the core of the international law enforcement system. If regime change is to be a legitimate goal, let us argue for that, agree on the criteria of legitimate statehood, and amend or replace the UN Charter accordingly.

So one cheer only for the fall of Hussein the tyrant. A second cheer can be kept in cold storage until credible links are established between his regime and international terrorism. And the third cheer would have been forthcoming if weapons of mass destruction had been found or used.

One final historical footnote: the Taliban too were welcomed into Kabul as liberators when they first went in, amid wild scenes of cheering and celebration. We know what happened next.

20

End of the old world disorder?

The Japan Times, 10 May 2003

Wars are cataclysmic events. Out of the destruction of major wars emerge new fault lines of international politics. To this extent, wars are the international, political equivalent of earthquakes, eruptions on the surface reflecting deeper underlying seismic shifts in the pattern of major-power relations.

The Cold War was unusual because of the longevity of the conflict and because of the peaceful manner in which it ended. The tectonic shifts ushered in by the realignment of forces after the Cold War were all the more significant, but they were hidden from view for an unusually long time because of the peaceful resolution.

It took the 11 September terrorist attacks to force the pace of change and sharpen the new post-Cold War contours of international politics. This new shape is more visible after the Iraq war.

Washington did not help its case for war against Iraqi President Saddam Hussein by issuing a confused mix of motives and explanations. In the resulting "noise" of diplomatic traffic, answers were not forthcoming to two crucial questions: Why Iraq, and why now? Any single answer to the first – such as known/suspected links to terrorism or to weapons of mass destruction – would always complicate attempts to answer the second, since people could instantly counter with more compelling cases of the same pathology.

For instance, with respect to weapons of mass destruction, while evidence of such remained elusive in Iraq, North Korea did almost everything but actually conduct a nuclear test. The glib conclusion drawn by the antiwar lobby, therefore, was that Washington's inconsistent response to the simultaneous crises showed two things: that Iraq did not possess usable nuclear weapons, and North Korea does not have oil.

Yet, glibness aside, Washington could have constructed a powerful case for its action on Iraq precisely by linking the two crises. We know that Hussein had pursued the nuclear option in the past, possessed and used biochemical weapons against his own people as well as Iran, and played a dangerous game of hide and seek with UN weapons inspectors for over a decade.

To the extent that we cannot be certain that North Korea has not already crossed the nuclear threshold, what options are available to the international community for dealing with Pyongyang without causing grave damage to ourselves?

Thus the two questions – why Iraq and why now – can be answered simultaneously and symbiotically. They also provide the justification for strategic preemption. Instead of proving that Hussein had "weapons of mass destruction," Washington found itself tied in knots and on shaky moral ground arguing that Hussein had to prove that he did not have them.

Preemption is not permitted under the UN Charter as it is not considered within the acknowledged right of self-defence. And this is precisely the point that got Australian Prime Minister John Howard into difficulty with some Asian neighbours after his musings after the terrorist carnage in Bali last October.

If preemption is strategically necessary and morally justified (why should an American president or an Australian prime minister wait for another mass murder, and be prohibited from taking preventive action?) but not legally permitted, then the existing framework of laws and rules – not the anticipatory military action – is defective.

The Iraq war proved to be mercifully swift and decisive. Now the most pressing task in Iraq is to stabilize the security situation; establish a transitional political authority; initiate the necessary steps for post-war reconstruction, peace-building and reconciliation; and embed these in durable institutions and structures that will be sufficiently resilient to survive the withdrawal of a foreign presence in due course. The larger goal in the region must be to assuage the humiliation inflicted on the collective Arab identity, deal with legitimate Palestinian grievances with the same mix of boldness and firmness shown in Iraq, and impress upon the Arab world in general the need for deep political, social and economic reforms.

There is also the larger question of the changing nature of threats in the modern world, the inadequacy of existing norms and laws in being able to address such threats, and thus the need for new "rules of the game" to replace them. The urgent task now is to devise an institutional framework that can marry prudent anticipatory self-defence by the democracies to the centuries-old dream of a world where force is put to the service of law that protects the innocent without shielding the criminals.

This is why the Iraq war has the potential to reshape the bases of world order in fundamental, profound and long-lasting ways. For, arguably, the Bush administration seeks to replace:

- self-defence (wars of necessity) with preventive aggression (wars of choice);
- the tried, tested and successful strategy of containment with the un-tried, untested, potentially destabilizing yet possibly unavoidable doc-trine of preemption;
- negative deterrence with positive compulsion;
- nonproliferation and disarmament, as represented in the Nuclear Non-Proliferation Treaty (NPT) package, with nonproliferation only;
- universal nonproliferation as per the NPT with differentiated nonpro-liferation, where the proliferating countries' relationship with the NPT is subordinated to their relations with the America. US-friendly countries like Israel are not on the list of countries of concern, while US-hostile countries are grouped into the "axis of evil" countries and US-ambivalent/neutral countries like India become objects of watchful caution;
- a multilateral system of global governance centred on the United Na-tions with a unilateral system of US preeminence;
- leadership by consent-cum-persuasion with leadership by command and control;
- the European search for a new world order, based on the Kantian tran-sition from barbarism to culture through liberal institutionalism, with the old world order discarded by Europe after centuries of increasingly destructive warfare, based on force of arms; and
- the Westphalian order of sovereign states, of equal status and legiti-macy, with a post-Westphalian order of one preeminent if virtuous power.

The long list of fundamental changes suggests that we shall continue to live in interesting times.

21

Humour's role in war survives

The Japan Times, 19 May 2003

After a lifetime as a student and teacher of international relations, I have been impressed by just how much of the essence of world affairs – not to mention the attention span of students and audiences – can be captured through pithy jokes. The recent Iraq war is no exception to this rule. (Although five years of living in Japan has also taught me that if there is simultaneous interpretation into Japanese, speakers are best advised to avoid jokes altogether. Humour does not easily translate across cultures, and by the time the interpreter has come to the punch line, the audience has long since lost any interest.)

One enduring lesson throughout human history, which has been reaffirmed in Iraq, is the manner in which all sides invoke divine blessing to their own call to arms even while denouncing the enemy as evil incarnate. This recalls a story from Baghdad during the days of the Caliphate. The Caliph (supreme ruler) was holding open court when a man was brought to him in chains, charged with claiming to be God.

Intrigued, the Caliph asked if it was indeed true that he claimed to be God. "Yes, Sire, it is."

"Why do you claim to be God?"

"Because I am, Sire."

"That's very interesting," said the Caliph. "Last week they brought someone to me in chains who claimed to be the messenger of God."

"And?" asked the prisoner.

"I had him executed," replied the Caliph.

"You did very well, Sire. He was an impostor: I had not sent him."

Two weeks into the recent war, the story goes, all of former Iraq leader

Saddam Hussein's doubles were summoned to a secret meeting in Baghdad. "I have good news and bad news," the security minister said to them. "The good news is that our dear leader is still alive, despite America's best efforts to bomb him. The bad news is that he lost an arm."

Shortly after the war came a story poking fun at today's instant experts. An American civilian is stopped on the streets of Baghdad by a friendly local and asked when he came to Iraq.

"Yesterday."

"How long will you be here?"

"I leave tomorrow."

"So short a visit to a country with such a long history. And what are you doing here?"

"I'm writing a book."

"Ah, how interesting. What is the book about?"

"It's called 'Iraq: Yesterday, Today and Tomorrow'."

One of the memorable phrases from the diplomatic wrangling leading up to the war was US Secretary of Defense Donald Rumsfeld's dismissive reference to France and Germany as "Old Europe." In response, some European commentators noted that, unlike these two old European countries, the new ones lacked a firmly rooted tradition of independent thought and action in foreign policy. Having been used to subservience towards the old Soviet Union, they were just as comfortable being deferential towards the new United States.

In the days of the independence struggle in India, one maharajah (king) became notorious for his fawning sycophancy towards the British authorities. No praise was high enough for them, no criticism too harsh for the Congress Party calling for the end to British rule. Come independence, the maharajah became equally obsequious towards the Congress government led by founding Prime Minister Jawaharlal Nehru. During a press conference, one journalist could not stomach it anymore and asked if His Highness wasn't the tiniest bit embarrassed by such blatant hypocrisy.

"What hypocrisy?" asked the maharajah.

"The switch from fawning on the British and hating the Congress, to fawning on the Congress after independence," said the journalist. "Doesn't this 180-degree change cause any shame?"

"Whatever do you mean," answered His Highness witheringly. "I haven't changed. The Raj has changed."

Similarly perhaps, "New Europe" has not changed; their centre of gravity has shifted from Moscow to Washington.

The French refusal to support the war brought forth a spate of anti-French jokes in the United States. One of my favourites was the line that "the French have always been there when they needed us." Except it seems more applicable to Washington's view of its alliances today. All allies should be on notice: America will be there when it needs you, on pain of being disciplined like the Mexicans or punished like the French. The fact that they may have fought alongside the Americans in recent wars, as in Kosovo and Afghanistan, will not prove sufficient insurance against retribution if they fail to support the United States again in any future war of its choice.

The forum that the French used to frustrate Washington was the United Nations. The unresolved deadlock in the Security Council was all too reminiscent of the cynical comment that the United Nations exists to give nations that are unable to do anything individually the forum to get together to decide that nothing can be done collectively. Except in this case Washington reversed it: If nothing is done collectively, the United States will show that successful action can still be undertaken individually.

And so the Americans have emerged even more contemptuous, as they see it, of the United Nations' indulgence of Hussein's rule and his history of prevarications. They could be forgiven for recalling the sad joke that if you kill one person, you get sent to court for trial; kill 20, you get sent to a mental asylum for treatment; kill 20,000, you get sent to Geneva for peace negotiations under UN auspices.

Yet in the weeks leading up to the war, the people of almost all countries demonstrated remarkable faith in the world organization as the proper forum for debating and authorizing any war in today's circumstances. And if there was justice in the world, Britain, Spain and the United States would be apologizing to the United Nations for all the calumny they heaped on it for refusing to accept that Hussein had operational weapons of mass destruction, ready to be used almost at instant notice. A famous Hollywood director once remarked that "the curious thing about Richard Wagner's music is that it ain't as bad as it sounds." Perhaps the same can be said of the United Nations.

The US irritation with the United Nations would most likely have been easier to assuage if the latter had not been proven to be right in opposing the war, at least on the grounds claimed during the six months of intractable and ultimately fruitless debate in the Security Council. The relationship between the United States and the United Nations is such that, if there is to be any kissing and making up, the latter will have to make most of the concessions.

Two bitter enemies come across each other on a narrow strip of road, too narrow for both to remain on the path at the point of crossing. The brawny one growls, "I don't give way to fools." The scrawny but brainy one responds, "That's all right, I do," and steps aside – a triumph of diplomacy over farce.

Sadly, the quality of diplomacy seems to have been seriously strained.

22

Contradictory US triumph

The Japan Times, 1 June 2003

An unusual, and thus intriguing, feature of the Iraq war is how both proponents and opponents feel passionately vindicated by what happened. The switch in justification – from finding and destroying Iraqi weapons of mass destruction before the war to the humanitarian liberation of Iraqis from a murderous tyrant afterward – is typical of both sides sticking firmly to their positions. It is also emblematic of a Washington policy that was full of major contradictions, so much so that almost every goal, laudable in itself, was fatally undermined by the means chosen.

Much as many people admire American values and wished to support them in the export of life, liberty and happiness to everyone else in the world, they remained hesitant and half-hearted about ousting Iraqi President Saddam Hussein because of doubts over the methods being employed.

The world remains sceptical about using war to preserve peace, and about the world's most powerful nuclear-armed country, which itself has seriously downgraded a number of key arms-control regimes seeking to check the role of nuclear weapons, using military force to prevent the pursuit of nuclear weapons by another country.

During the Iraq war India's foreign minister mused that Pakistan could be considered an even more fit case for preemption than Iraq. Indonesia is the most recent to have caught the virus of military solutions to conflicts, photo-op assaults in glorious Technicolor and "embedded" journalists accompanying offensive troops to gratify citizens' appetite for virtual reality combat.

These contradictions, however, are more apparent than real, and can be resolved. Many people mistakenly believe that the United Nations cannot, as a matter of principle, endorse the use of military force in world affairs. This is simply wrong. The United Nations was built on the assumption that sometimes force may have to be threatened, and even used, to preserve, restore and guarantee peace.

Chapter 7 of the UN Charter is devoted to military enforcement by the international community acting collectively. And Iraq had, and still has, solemn written obligations under the Nuclear Non-Proliferation Treaty (NPT) and various UN resolutions to forswear nuclear weapons – obligations that are qualitatively different from the intentionally weaker ones of the five nuclear powers in the NPT schema.

The remaining contradictions are more difficult to resolve, at least to the satisfaction of non-Americans. How do we promote the prospects of cooperation with international agencies by regimes under suspicion of engaging in clandestine activities with regard to prohibited classes of weapons, if such cooperation leads first to an enfeebled self-defence capability and then to an armed attack?

How is it possible to achieve victory in the war on international terrorism directed at American targets by inciting a deeper hatred of US foreign policy around the world? Most informed observes of the Arab world seem to agree that the sight of American forces occupying Baghdad will spur more terrorism, not less, especially while the open Palestinian wound continues to fester on the collective Arab body politic.

Although we do, at long last, have a roadmap to peace there, cynics could be excused for wondering whether the recent terrorist attacks on soft foreign targets in Saudi Arabia have been blamed on Iran-based al-Qaeda operatives in part as a means of deflecting attention away from the dramatic evidence of the survival of the international terrorist network, which would be a contradiction of claimed successes in the war on terror.

It is difficult to see how one country can enforce UN resolutions by defying the authority of the world body, denigrating it as irrelevant and belittling its role in reconstruction efforts after the war. In a Gallup poll of 45 countries released 13 May, most agreed that the United Nations has been seriously damaged by recent events and wanted it to play a bigger role in post-war Iraq.

Nor is it possible to promote the rule of law and the role of international law in world affairs and to act as the world's policeman by hollowing out some of the most important parts of international law that restrict the right to go to war except in self-defence or when authorized by the United Nations. In the Iraq war, established institutions and conventions for ensuring that force is legitimately exercised were set aside by a power supremely confident of its might.

If the price is right, one can always find lawyers to argue any case. It is a big leap in logic to say that any claim by partisan lawyers is automatically correct. On this basis, we would never have any verdict in domestic legal systems. If a war of choice against a country that posed no conceivable security threat to any other country is legal, then international law has no place anymore in governing warfare.

Law serves to mediate relations between the rich and the poor, the weak and the powerful, by acting as a constraint on capricious behaviour and setting limits on the arbitrary exercise of power. If the normative restraints of the legal code of behaviour are overthrown by the eagle-eyed predators of the international jungle, will not others, guided by the age-old instinct of self-preservation, seek recourse to whatever weapons of deterrence they can acquire by hook or crook?

The most problematic contradiction is in relation to the professed goal of establishing democracy in Iraq and using it as a beacon to promote political freedoms across the Arab world. How does one instil democracy in an inhospitable terrain by punishing friends and allies – in the home continent of the founding values of Western civilization – who dared to exercise their democratic right to dissent from a war whose justification still remains contentious, while rewarding dictators who lent ready support?

What answer is there for those who claim that aggression abroad was matched by repression at home, with serious cutbacks to many liberties that US citizens, residents and visitors alike had come to take for granted for decades?

Democracy might also be the one outcome that Americans cannot afford in Iraq. Given Iraq's demographic composition, genuinely free elections could bring a Shiite-dominated Islamist regime aligned to Iran. We have already heard chants of "No to Saddam, No to America, Yes to Islam," as the Shiite clergy moved quickly to fill the power vacuum in the wake of Hussein's downfall.

As with the Palestinians vis-a-vis their leader Yasser Arafat, the Iraqis will be permitted to exercise democratic freedoms, but within clearly set limits: on pain of consequences. Again, it is certainly useful to be able to blame this on Iranian interference in Iraqi affairs.

Given this set of internal contradictions between ends and means, is it any wonder that, in the 45-nation Gallup poll, world opinion against the war barely shifted even after the swift and decisive victory of the United States and its allies, and after footage of Iraqis celebrating the downfall of Hussein? Over two-thirds of the people of France, Germany, Greece and Spain still hold that military action was wrong; the majority in almost all countries believe the world to be less safe as a result of the war; and most countries think the United States is much too keen to use military force.

Of course, you have to understand and believe in democracy to care about what people actually think and want.

23

Why India said "no" to US

The Japan Times, 17 July 2003

Those who think little of the United Nations are constantly puzzled by the authority it continues to exert for many others around the world. On Monday, India decided against sending a major contingent of troops to Iraq because the operation would be outside the UN mandate, thereby reconfirming Secretary-General Kofi Annan's point about the unique legitimacy of the world organization. Having initially been sympathetic to Washington's request to contribute an army division (some 17,000 troops) for post-war security duty in Iraq – in particular to stabilize the situation in northern Iraq – New Delhi in the end, "on balance of considerations," said no.

The very keen desire to consolidate improved relations with Washington was insufficient to overcome deep domestic divisions about the stability of the theatre of operations being assigned to India and the financial costs of an operation.

India was attractive to Washington for a number of reasons. One of the largest troop contributors to UN peacekeeping operations, the Indian Army has adequate manpower readily available and trained for peacekeeping, experience in all types of climate and terrain, and military capabilities ranging from mechanized operations to dismounted infantry, engineers and humanitarian support.

In the scope and sophistication of its democracy and the size and professionalism of its armed forces, India is closer to some of the Western powers. But as a very poor country, it is acutely representative of developing, formerly colonized countries.

As a rule, India has favoured authorization for the international use of force by representative international organizations or bodies, preferably the United Nations. Its motives for participating in UN peace operations are a mix of idealism (commitment to internationalism) and pragmatic calculations (pursuit of national interests, in particular the claim to permanent membership of the Security Council).

A well-crafted policy exists to decide India's participation in overseas military missions. The Ministry of External Affairs determines the international political acceptability of a proposed peacekeeping mission and whether it serves national interests. The Ministry of Defence examines the request from the perspective of domestic political acceptability. The Armed Forces Headquarters examines the operational requirements.

The political and military risk analysis used to determine India's participation in peace operations has included questions of national security interests, whether the host country has a history of friendly relations with India (as Iraq did), the likelihood of Indian troops becoming involved in sectarian strife in which one or more parties is Islamic, the precedent-setting dangers of violating a host country's sovereignty and territorial integrity, the extent of regional and global support for the operation, UN command and control, a clear mandate and time frame, and financial arrangements for compensating troop-contributing countries.

The one clear advantage to India of saying yes would have been the gratitude of the Bush administration, which has made it a very public point to reward risk-taking military partners and punish recalcitrant allies. Paradoxically, as the situation on the ground in Iraq remained unstable, the wish of the administration for visible support from a broader international coalition grew even as the resolve of others to contribute was weakened. The failure to find weapons of mass destruction has also sapped the will to help Washington. The war enthusiasts are described as pursuing a faith-based approach to intelligence: we know the answers, just give us the evidence to back us up.

India's powerful Deputy Prime Minister and Home Minister L.K. Advani joined Finance Minister Jaswant Singh in supporting the deployment of an Indian division to Iraq, but changed his mind as the extent and persistence of domestic opposition became clear. National Security Adviser Brajesh Mishra too shifted into the uncertain and probably opposed camp. Foreign Minister Yaswant Sinha was said to be ambivalent, with Defence Minister George Fernandes opposed. In the crucial meeting of the Cabinet committee on security on Monday, Prime Minister Atal Behari Vajpayee sided with the opponents and the matter was settled.

Almost all political parties voiced strong opposition to sending Indian troops to Iraq to serve under US command. The memory of Indian soldiers having done London's "dirty work" in the far-flung outposts of the

British Empire continues to exert a powerful pull against participation in modern-day "Empire Lite" ventures.

Some Indian business firms could see profit opportunities if construction contracts were to come their way with Indian military operations in Iraq. But former prime minister I.K. Gujral scoffed that "there is something un-Indian and undignified in becoming a subcontractor to the Pentagon in order to become a sub-contractor to American multinationals."

Kashmir was as much a pull as a push factor in the decision. There is anxiety, on the one hand, that if India says no and Pakistan says yes, then Washington's fault tolerance of Pakistani behaviour will be strengthened. On the other hand, India has enough problems in its sole Muslim-majority province without aggravating the situation by taking part in what has widely been seen in the Islamic world as an unjustified assault on a hapless Muslim country. India's "no" will likely turn up the heat on Pakistan to stand firm against the US request as well, sharpening Gen. Pervez Musharraf's painfully acute dilemma of wanting to please the Americans without antagonizing his Muslim population.

New Delhi concluded that its army does not need the sort of divisiveness in Indian society and politics that would be guaranteed by sending troops to Iraq. With Washington reportedly unwilling to underwrite the financial costs of Indian participation, New Delhi balked at having to pay to get its soldiers shot at in a risky, possibly open-ended, overseas venture.

This could yet change if Washington could bring itself to seek and accept UN Security Council blessing for a peace operation in Iraq under UN command. Participation in UN peace operations is neither a politically contentious issue in India, nor a constitutionally complicated exercise. It has not been a divisive subject of public debate. The larger lesson for Washington should be to be careful not to trash the United Nations and diminish its authority, for the organization is often useful in picking up the pieces after others have shattered the fragile edifice of world order.

24

Chrétien was right: It's time to redefine a "just war"

The Globe and Mail, 22 July 2003

The 1990s was a challenging decade. Our consciences were shocked by atrocities from Rwanda to Bosnia and beyond, and by the price that innocent men, women and children paid because of the world's failure to rise to such challenges.

Though the terrorist attacks of 11 September shifted attention to the war on terrorism, the debate about the need to intervene in sovereign countries for the purpose of human protection has not gone away. Indeed, since coalition forces in Iraq have failed to find any weapons of mass destruction, human protection has become the only remaining significant justification for the US-led war on the dictator Saddam Hussein.

But does Iraq meet the test of "humanitarian intervention"? See for yourself by taking a look at the report, "The Responsibility to Protect," by the International Commission on Intervention and State Sovereignty (dubbed "R2P"). Prime Minister Jean Chrétien tried valiantly to promote this report at the recent Progressive Governance Summit in England. He ran into difficulty because some at the conference feared that the concept could be used to justify the war on Iraq.

This is ironic, for most ICISS commissioners (I was one) would argue that the Iraq war would not have met our criteria for justifying intervention.

Because it's easy to label a war as a "humanitarian intervention" – deflecting critics who don't want to be cast as "anti-humanitarian" – we recommended a change in terminology. It's important to focus attention on needs of victims, including the prevention and follow-up assistance components of external action (issues that are becoming major concerns in post-war Iraq).

As such, we found it useful to reconceptualize sovereignty, viewing it not as an absolute term of authority but as a kind of responsibility. State authorities are responsible for the functions of protecting the safety and lives of citizens, and accountable for their acts of commission and omission in international as well as national forums. While the state has the primary responsibility to protect its citizens, the responsibility of the broader community of states is activated when a particular state either is unwilling or unable to fulfil its responsibility to protect; or is itself the perpetrator of crimes or atrocities; or where populations living outside a particular state are directly threatened by actions taking place there.

We sought to define thresholds when atrocities are so grave, they clearly require armed international intervention. Such thresholds are crossed when large-scale loss of life or ethnic cleansing is occurring or is about to occur (this rule is not retroactive, and does not justify intervention now for atrocities committed years ago).

As well, we argued that all military interventions must be subject to four precautionary principles: right intention, last resort, proportional means and reasonable prospects. Iraq would likely have failed on all four principles.

Intervention for human protection purposes occurs so that those condemned to die in fear may live in hope instead. The goal is not to wage war on a state in order to destroy it and eliminate its statehood, but to protect victims of atrocities inside the state, to embed the protection in reconstituted institutions after the intervention, and then to withdraw all foreign troops.

Given the enormous normative presumption against the use of deadly force to settle international quarrels, who has the right to authorize such force?

Even if we agree that military intervention may sometimes be necessary and unavoidable in order to protect innocent people from life-threatening danger, key questions remain about the international authority that can override national sovereignty.

R2P came down firmly on the side of the central role of the United Nations as the indispensable font of international authority and the irreplaceable forum for authorizing international military enforcement. While its work can be supplemented by regional organizations acting within their own jurisdictions, only the United Nations can build, consolidate and use military force in the name of the international community.

Our choice is no longer between intervention and non-intervention, but between ad hoc, or rules-based, intervention. If we are going to get any sort of consensus in advance of crises requiring urgent responses, including military intervention, the principles outlined in "Responsibility to Protect" point the way forward. If hostile governments and critics can move beyond their reflexive suspicion of the very word "intervention," they'll find that R2P contains the safeguards they need with respect to threshold causes, precautionary principles, lawful authorization and operational doctrine.

25

Anti-nuke regime crumbling

The Japan Times, 24 October 2003

Speaking on the opening day of the UN General Assembly's disarmament committee on 6 October, Ambassador Sergio Querioz Duarte of Brazil noted that "to attain a nuclear-weapon-free world, it is vital to prevent nuclear proliferation, and at the same time, it is imperative to promote nuclear disarmament." The chairman of the committee, Ambassador Jarmo Sareva of Finland, listed the following as the problems faced by the international community: the acquisition by additional states of nuclear weapons, allegations of still more trying to get them, the failure by those that already have them to eliminate their stocks and the development of new weapons that do not fall under any existing international regime – space-based weapons, for example.

On the following day, US Assistant Secretary of State Stephen Rademaker accused the committee of being stuck in obsolete Cold War-era thinking that had produced "years of disappointing drift and growing irrelevance." What it should address, he said, are non-compliance with treaty obligations and efforts to prevent weapons of mass destruction from falling into the hands of terrorists.

Thus the subject of nuclear proliferation, arms control and disarmament is back on the international agenda with a vengeance. The lengthening list of proliferation-sensitive concerns includes the embarrassing failure to find weapons of mass destruction in Iraq, strident bellicosity from Pyongyang proclaiming a weaponized nuclear capability that outsiders are sceptical of but dare not discount totally, concerns expressed by the International Atomic Energy Agency about Iran's nuclear program, and reports that Saudi Arabia may be contemplating an off-the-shelf purchase of nuclear weapons.

The goal of containing the genie of nuclear weapons was unexpectedly successful for three decades from 1968 to 1998, but has suffered serious setbacks since then. The success rested on three pillars, each of which has been crumbling in the last two to five years: norms, treaties and coercion.

Norms are efficient mechanisms for regulating social behaviour from the family and village to the global setting. They enable us to pursue goals, challenge assertions and justify actions. One of the most powerful norms since 1945 has been the taboo on the use of nuclear weapons. Even the United States and the former Soviet Union accepted defeat on the battlefield by non-nuclear rivals rather than break the antinuclear taboo.

In May 1998, India and Pakistan conducted nuclear tests. In doing so, they broke no treaty, for neither had signed the Nuclear Non-Proliferation Treaty (NPT). But they violated the global antinuclear norm, and were roundly criticized for doing so. By now they are increasingly being accepted back into the fold as de facto nuclear powers, which weakens the antinuclear norm still further.

A norm cannot control the behaviour of those who reject its legitimacy. India had argued for decades that the most serious breaches of the antinuclear norm were being committed by the five nuclear powers, who simply disregarded their disarmament obligations under the NPT. The imbalance of reporting, monitoring and compliance mechanisms between the nonproliferation and disarmament clauses of the NPT, India insisted, had in effect created nuclear apartheid.

Of late Washington has retreated from a series of arms control and disarmament agreements, including the antiballistic missile, nuclear nonproliferation and comprehensive test-ban treaties. In doing so, Washington contributes to a worsening of the proliferation challenge. It is difficult to convince others of the futility of nuclear weapons when some demonstrate their utility by the very fact of hanging on to them and developing new doctrines for their use.

It would be wrong to single out just the United States. It defies history, common sense and logic to believe that a group of five countries can keep a permanent monopoly on any class of weaponry. The non-fulfilment of treaty obligations by the nuclear powers weakens the efficacy of the antinuclear norm in controlling the threat of proliferation. The five permanent members of the UN Security Council – who are the five nuclear powers – then have to resort to measures of coercion ranging from diplomatic and economic to military. But relying solely on coercion with little basis any longer on norms (morality) and treaties (legality) in turn gives rise to fresh problems.

First, it is simply not credible to threaten friends and allies who neither accept the validity of the norm nor can be accused of breaching treaties they have not signed. Thus US policy has shifted de facto from universal nonproliferation based on the NPT to differentiated proliferation based on relations of the regimes in question with Washington. US-friendly countries like Israel will be ignored, US-hostile "rogue regimes" like North Korea will be threatened and punished.

Second, however, such a dramatic deterioration of the security environment hardens the determination of the "rogues" to acquire the most lethal weapons in order to check armed attacks they fear will be launched by the United States. Just as Iraq as a hotbed of terrorism became a consequence more than a cause of war, so proliferation of nuclear weapons may result from the war. Some countries, not the least North Korea, have concluded that only nuclear weapons can deter Washington from unilateral wars of choice.

Third, the reality of contemporary threats – a virtual nuclear-weapons capability that can exist inside nonproliferation regimes and be crossed at too short a notice for international organizations to be able to react defensively in time, and nonstate actors who are outside the jurisdiction and control of multilateral agreements whose signatories are limited to states – means that significant gaps exist in the legal and institutional framework to combat them. Recognizing this, a group of like-minded countries has launched a Proliferation Security Initiative (PSI), which recently involved the military and special forces of 11 nations taking part in joint interdiction and intercept exercises in international waters near Australia.

The goal is to be able to interdict air, sea and land cargo linked to weapons of mass destruction on the basis of a set of agreed principles. Its premise is that the proliferation of such weapons deserves to be criminalized by the civilized community of nations. It signifies a broad partnership of countries that, using their own national laws and resources, will coordinate actions to halt shipments of dangerous technologies and materiel.

Questions remain about the legal basis for searching and interdicting ships in international waters. It runs the risk of being seen as a vigilante approach to nonproliferation by an 11-strong posse led by a self-appointed world sheriff. Yet the very fact that the PSI has been launched and combined exercises have been held signals a new determination to overcome an unsatisfactory state of affairs, and may therefore act as a deterrent. Moreover, the involvement of Australia and Japan alongside the United States in the Pacific, plus another eight European countries (Britain, France, Germany, Italy, the Netherlands, Poland, Portugal and Spain), signals a welcome return to multilateralism in trying to deal with the problem. But there is a long way to go before the PSI develops into a robust counter-proliferation strategy in which there is general confidence.

In sum, there was great merit in relying on an integrated strategy of norms, treaties and coercion to keep the nuclear threat in check. The three pillars are mutually reinforcing in holding up the structure of arms control.

26

UNSC: Reforming the United Nations

The Daily Yomiuri, 24 October 2003

As the world marks United Nations Day Friday, the world body's future and prestige is under scrutiny as never before. Speaking to the UN General Assembly on 23 September, UN Secretary-General Kofi Annan noted that "we have come to a fork in the road ... a moment no less decisive than 1945 itself, when the United Nations was founded." Accordingly, he has decided to set up a panel of eminent people to make recommendations on significant reforms for the United Nations.

The subject of most interest to the Japanese is the structural reform of the Security Council. For any international enforcement action to be efficient, it must be legitimate; for it to be legitimate, it must be in conformity with international law; for it to conform to international law, it must be consistent with the Charter of the United Nations.

The Security Council is the core of the international law enforcement system. While some countries and commentators chafe at the sorry performance of the Council and attribute its declining role and legitimacy to ineffectiveness, others blame its declining effectiveness on its diminished legitimacy due to its increasingly unrepresentative composition.

But what exactly does "representative" mean in this context? Does the Security Council gain or lose legitimacy if it is representative of governments who do not represent their own people?

All countries agree on the need to reform the Security Council, and almost all countries agree that Japan and India should be among the permanent members. But there is no majority support for any one concrete package with regard to the number of permanent and elected members, and the veto power.

Permanent membership adds to the international influence and prestige of countries. The most obvious, immediate and compelling argument for Japan to become a permanent member is the size of its financial contribution. At 19.5 percent of the total budget, Japan pays more than four of the permanent members combined (14.7 percent); only the United States pays more (22 percent).

The United Nations was helpful in reintegrating Japan into the international community after the misfortunes of World War II. But that is history. In effect, Japan is subject to taxation without representation. In the real world, governments have to make hard choices between different spending priorities. It is difficult to see how the people and government of Japan can put up with this anomaly forever; Japan is not an automatic teller machine for the United Nations.

Japan also carries a considerable burden with respect to voluntary contributions to other parts of the UN system, including the United Nations University (UNU). As the only part of the UN family to have its global headquarters in Asia, UNU's symbolic importance is far greater than its size would suggest. And Japan has been the host and chief financial supporter of UNU.

Japan's claim to permanent membership does not rest on the single criterion of chequebook diplomacy. The fact that the existing five permanent members are also the five nuclear powers is particularly unfortunate, as part of the UN mandate is to promote nuclear arms control and disarmament. The formula "P5=N5" (Permanent-5=Nuclear-5) is damaging to the legitimacy and authority of the United Nations. Adding Japan as a permanent member would be just reward for its voluntary non-nuclear status and break the identification of permanent membership of the Security Council with possession of nuclear weapons.

Similarly, the Security Council also has the responsibility to promote reductions in conventional arms, yet its P5 account for almost 90 percent of the world's arms sales. Again, Japan is an exceptionally good international citizen in eschewing arms sales as a matter of deliberate state policy.

Instead, Japan has actively pursued humane civilian internationalism in its foreign policy, starting with foreign aid and culminating in recent years in the promotion of human security. Japan and the United States are the world's more or less equal leading aid donors.

Japan is a model UN member state in other important respects as well. It is the success story par excellence of a country rebuilt and rehabilitated after the ravages and ruination of a devastating major war. It is a liberal economy, a major trading nation and a mature democracy with a vast and fully literate civil society.

Most recently, since its first participation in a peacekeeping operation in Cambodia in 1992, Japan has been drawn into peace and security contributions of increasing magnitude and spreading geographic range.

Where some countries have doubts about Japan's credentials, it is based on one of two considerations. Some worry that Japan lacks the capacity to articulate an independent voice on important security issues.

The United States already dominates the UN system; why give it a guaranteed extra vote in the Security Council? Maybe permanent membership would give Japan that extra bit of confidence to be able to disagree on some issues while still being there alongside Washington whenever it matters the most.

The more serious worry is that the industrial countries are already overrepresented on the Security Council. This is where India's claims become attractive, as well as its billion-strong population, vibrant democracy, long history of major contributions to PKOs and de facto nuclear power status.

Happily, no one is calling for a choice between Japan and India. After all, Asia accounts for more than half the world's population. So a total of three out of 10 permanent members would not be out of line for the super-continent. Both Japan and India are likely to maximize their chances of success if they work with rather than against each other. Indeed, active collaboration with the other lead contenders could help to build momentum through a powerful global coalition.

As Secretary-General Annan remarked, "The difficulty of reaching agreement does not excuse failure to do so." The difficulty for him is that he cannot tell member states what to do on matters of policy. This is a decision to be made in the national capitals of the world, not in the Secretariat of the United Nations.

The formula of an independent and prestigious panel, even if appointed by the secretary-general, allows him to short-circuit the difficulty. The Iraq war highlighted the gravity of structural inadequacies and the urgency of reform; the panel could be the circuit breaker in the stalemate.

27

Reforming the United Nations

The Japan Times, 8 December 2003

The United Nations is our collective instrument for organizing a volatile and dangerous world on a more predictable and orderly basis than would be possible without the existence of the organization. As the year that saw war in Iraq draws to a close, the future and prestige of the United Nations is under scrutiny as never before. It is seen far too often as a bloated, high-cost, junket-loving irrelevance to the real needs and concerns of the nations of the world. Yet most people still look to the United Nations as our best hope for a shared future, especially if it could somehow be reformed to reflect today's needs and realities.

Speaking to the UN General Assembly on 23 September, Secretary-General Kofi Annan noted that "we have come to a fork in the road ... a moment no less decisive than 1945 itself, when the United Nations was founded." Accordingly, he announced his intention to form a panel of eminent persons to make recommendations on significant political and structural reforms to bring the United Nations into line with current threats and challenges to peace and security. The 16-member panel, announced subsequently, includes Sadako Ogata of Japan.

In most peoples' minds, talk of UN reform implies either the need to tackle the problem of a polemical, wasteful organization, staffed by self-serving, overpaid bureaucrats who provide little more than a talk-fest, or the need to make surgical reforms of a Security Council that is 1945 vintage in composition, opaque in its workings and obstructionist in its effect. The first need is caricature, the second exaggerated. But perceptions matter, and there is enough need for reform for harsh perceptions to persist and damage the organization.

In a number of key meetings during and after World War II, world leaders drew up rules to govern international behaviour and established a network of institutions, centred on the United Nations, to work together for the common good. Both the rules and institutions – the system of global governance with the United Nations as the core – are under serious challenge. On the one hand, Annan noted, the Iraq war could set a precedent for the "proliferation of the unilateral and lawless use of force." On the other hand, he asked, to what extent might states be resorting to unilateral instruments because of a loss of faith in "the adequacy and effectiveness of the rules and instruments" at their disposal?

This is why, he concluded, we need to take a hard look both at fundamental policy issues and structural changes that may be necessary for the United Nations to win back and retain the confidence of peoples and governments.

The central doctrinal dispute concerns the Westphalian fiction, which pervades the UN structure and workings, that sovereign states are equal in effectiveness, status and legitimacy. In reality, states are not of equal worth and significance, neither militarily, economically, politically nor morally. Some countries indeed can only be called criminal states. Their membership of the United Nations – let alone their presence on the Security Council or the image of their leaders being feted as honoured guests when they address the General Assembly – is an affront to the ideals and values symbolized by the august organization. The commitment to "We, the peoples of the world" in the opening words of the UN Charter could be profoundly subversive of many governments of the world who take their countries' seat at the United Nations.

Equally, though, there is a contradiction between the roles of the five permanent members as the chief guardians of international security and their status as the major arms exporters of the world. To be able to see others' double standards with ease while rationalizing one's own is a common human failing.

In turn, this affects the discussion of structural reforms. All countries agree on the need to reform the Security Council, but there is no majority support for any one concrete package with regard either to the numbers of permanent and elected members or to veto power.

While some chafe at the sorry performance of the Security Council and attribute its declining role and legitimacy to ineffectiveness, others blame this on its increasingly unrepresentative composition. How can Africa and Latin America, or the Islamic world not have any permanent members? For that matter, how can Asia, home to more than half the world's total population, have only one permanent seat? How can Japan, which pays more to the UN coffers than France, Britain, China and Russia combined (four of the five existing permanent members), not be a permanent member? And does the Security Council gain or lose legitimacy if it is representative of governments who do not represent their own people?

The answers to these questions are coloured by self-interest on all sides, with the collective interest of the international community being relegated to secondary status. Those determined to obstruct any meaningful reform have worked together more cleverly and more energetically than those who wish to promote major structural reform.

Some believe that the more urgent and feasible part of the reform agenda is to tackle the excessive politicization and trivialization of the work of the General Assembly rather than the Security Council. If the Council is the geopolitical centre of gravity of the United Nations, then the secretary-general is the custodian of the world's conscience and the personification of the international interest, and the Assembly is the normative centre of gravity.

Its work is notorious for a fixation on procedures and preference for point-scoring and finger-pointing over problem-solving, with little sense of custodial responsibility for the world. The Council has had to expand its agenda and workload not because of imperial ambitions, but because of the Assembly's profoundly diminished capacity to make meaningful decisions.

The mirror opposite of this are those who insist that reforms in the Assembly must not even be addressed until the Council's reform agenda is completed. They are suspicious of talk of Assembly reform as a diversionary ploy, an alibi for inaction on the Council front.

A third group acknowledges the need for Council reform, but argues that the task of reforming the Assembly is equally urgent and must not be held hostage to what happens in the Council: The Assembly belongs to us, and we should not let our agenda be determined by the games big powers play in the Council. Instead, let us get our own act together, and the prestige and authority of the Assembly will rise in correspondence with its successful revitalization.

The General Assembly is the only universal forum in which all countries have an equal voice. Its budgetary powers give it considerable authority over the work of the organization. But its contribution has been diminishing due to some serious flaws. It must rationalize its agenda, reform its workings and clarify its responsibilities vis-a-vis other UN bodies. As the one body that houses the divided fragments of humanity, it must lead the way, and not be content simply to follow.

28

2003: Worst and best of times for UN

The Japan Times, 8 January 2004

Twelve months ago, the international community heaved a sigh of relief as the major powers appeared to reach a compromise on how to manage Iraq. But Washington's determination to act on its own cut short the role of UN weapons inspectors and challenged the very notion that the organization has a role to play in issues of peace and security.

Today, the international scene is much altered. Bogged down in Iraq, Washington is relying on multilateral processes to address threats of nuclear proliferation in North Korea and Iran. It also has backed down on protectionist tariffs on steel imports condemned by the World Trade Organization.

The capture of Saddam Hussein provided welcome respite, but foreign-policy coherence is still missing in action in Washington. The situation in Iraq, a product of a post-9/11 reaction aggravated by hubris, offers no attractive short-term options. And in the long term, as Lord Keynes remarked, we are all dead.

In the Middle East's core conflict, meanwhile, the most promising initiative came from unofficial representatives of Israelis and Palestinians in the form of the Geneva Accord. Increasing discussion of a single-state solution – involving the Jewish and Arab inhabitants and territories of Israel, the West Bank and Gaza – has generated a sense among many that time and demographic developments are making agreement more urgent.

The war on terrorism is too narrow. A strategy undermining support for terrorism by addressing sources of discontent is a necessary complement to actions aimed at taking out terrorists themselves. The war on terrorism must also delve into politics – redress group grievances and assuage collective humiliation – while fighting in the back streets, deserts and mountain valleys.

The year was a sobering one for the European Union, split over both foreign and economic policy and unable to agree on constitutional arrangements. For those who believe a united Europe on foreign policy would be a stabilizing force in international relations, the sight of Britain and France at each other's throats in the Security Council (with Spain and Germany dug in behind) was depressing. No less striking was Franco-German willingness to ride roughshod over the EU's economic stability pact because of domestic imperatives.

The world eagerly looks forward to Japan's continuing emergence as a force to be reckoned with in the councils of world diplomacy. Can it shake off burdens of historical guilt and a propensity to be the automatic teller machine for grandiose UN and US schemes to help repair major damage caused by nature and man alike? The dearth of bold and skilled international relations professionals to fashion an independent and self-confident foreign policy weighs down Prime Minister Junichiro Koizumi's admirable attempt to push Japan into the 21st century.

Asia, particularly regional giants China and India, continues to see growth amid dizzying disparities. Economic expansion has largely displaced security concerns, but terrorism remains a threat – and now a more openly acknowledged one.

The year did little to counter the growing impression of China's ascendance as Asia's major political and diplomatic player. It took a lead role in trying to resolve the nuclear standoff on the Korean Peninsula; established common cause with India and Brazil at the failed Cancun talks to challenge EU-US hegemony in global trade negotiations; kept relations with Washington on an even keel; and sent a citizen into space.

India maintained its tradition of rambunctious democracy but seems finally to have broken from its record of dismal economic performance. By year's end, there was genuine hope in the air that Indian Prime Minister Atal Behari Vajpayee and Pakistani President Pervez Musharraf were getting serious about trying to cut a deal on Kashmir.

Africa had a mixed year. The African Union selected an impressive chairman in Alpha Oumar Konare, former president of Mali. South African President Thabo Mbeki reversed his opposition to science-based treatment of the AIDS pandemic, while international pharmaceutical companies belatedly moved to make such treatment more accessible. Amid the combination of sanctions, UN inspections and hard negotiations, Libya decided to abandon the pursuit of weapons of mass destruction.

However, progress has been slow in the application of the African-generated New Economic Program for Africa's Development, which favours improved governance and greater democracy. Some African leaders are unwilling to confront Zimbabwe's march to destitution and violence under the dictatorial Robert Mugabe.

Latin America continues to disappoint, to a much lesser degree, on economic and democratic performance. Mexico's President Vicente Fox is frustrated by Congress and weighed down by his own mistakes. Brazil's President Luiz (Lula) da Silva, enjoying a domestic honeymoon, is forging an intriguing diplomatic coalition with India and South Africa. Regionwide free trade seems a receding mirage as the United States picks off successive partners for bilateral deals.

For the United Nations, it was the worst of times and the best of times. The advocates of war condemned it for failing to enforce Iraqi compliance with UN resolutions; opponents faulted it for failing to punish the aggressors. The deep tears in the fabric of international society in 2003 took its toll on the credibility of the United Nations, yet people still look to it as the forum for global problem-solving.

The Iraq war damaged the three great institutions of the last half century – the European Union, North Atlantic Treaty Organization and the United Nations. In addition, preemptive war is now a featured fare on Washington's policy menu.

The United Nations and the United States share an interest in isolating and defeating terrorism – not each other – and in promoting democracy, human rights and the rule of law. May the new year see much progress on each of these.

Note

Article co-authored with David Malone. Mr. Malone is a former Canadian ambassador to the United Nations and has served as the president of the International Peace Academy in New York. He is now Canada's high commissioner to India.

29

Neighbours don diplomatic pads

The Australian, 12 March 2004

Cricket is the secular religion uniting Indians and Pakistanis in the intensity of their passion for it. When the teams assemble for the opening one-day match in Karachi tomorrow – which marks the start of India's first full cricket tour of Pakistan in 15 years – work will come to a stop. Millions will tune in to radio and television. And the bustling teashops will become the nerve-centres of feverish discussion on the esoteric intricacies of every move, ball, stroke and umpiring decision.

Now, to say that the India-Pakistan rivalry is fierce is an understatement. When India last visited Pakistan, for example, fans threw stones at the Indian players during the match in Karachi. And four years ago, Hindu militants dug up the pitch in New Delhi to protest against the Pakistani team's visit.

Given the troubled and sometimes violent history of cricketing relations in the subcontinent, among the most anxious spectators will be the two governments. The hope is that India's cricket tour of Pakistan will help bring together two nations who have fought three wars since they became independent from Britain in 1947.

Sports, after all, has always been an integral part of politics. The Romans recognized this in their gladiatorial contests. Hitler exploited the Berlin Olympics in 1936. And winning the rugby union World Cup in 1995 was a powerful boost to post-apartheid South Africa's triumphal return to the international sporting scene.

Australia and India recently concluded one of the most exciting series of Test cricket in memory. Written off on arrival by most commentators as a pushover despite their abundant talent, Indian captain Sourav Ganguly and his team ended the series with glowing testimonials to their fluent strokeplay, fighting spirit and good humour.

In this, the Indian cricketers symbolize the new India. Rich talent is married to burning ambition. No longer is India prepared to concede ground to anyone else. Instead, it is keen to take on the world and beat it at its own game on its home territory.

India's software industry is closely associated with the new "can do" spirit: isn't it wonderful to see the United States seeking protection against newly competitive India? But clearly the spirit, the self-belief in victory and success, is proving to be infectious. India's youth see their future on the global stage; they are not content to survive behind the protective cocoon of home advantage.

The same phenomenon of risk-taking entrepreneurship has led New Delhi to approve the series with Pakistan on the eve of a general election in India in April-May. The decision in favour of the Indian team's tour of Pakistan was announced on 15 February, just two days before officials began the initial round of exploratory peace talks in Islamabad.

The election strategy of the ruling Bharatiya Janata Party is to exploit the sense of wellbeing that is almost palpable in India these days.

The performance of the cricket team in Australia contributed to the "feel good" factor. Some cabinet ministers were worried that a terrorist attack on Indian cricketers on Pakistani soil, or a loss to Pakistan, would destroy the sense of wellbeing and self-confidence. Others argued that a tour would underscore the government's claim that cross-border terrorism had declined and India-Pakistan relations were being normalized.

Cancellation of the series, planned after a lapse of many years, would have inflicted a serious financial penalty on the country's cricket board. India's cricket-mad public (and betting industry?) was strongly in favour of the tour going ahead.

At the crucial meeting of BJP heavyweights on 14 February, foreign affairs specialists were the ones voting yes, although reaching out to the sizeable Muslim vote must also have been a calculation. The announcement the next day made it clear that prime minister Atal Behari Vajpayee's wishes had prevailed for the tour to proceed.

The Indian team can still collapse with a breathtaking suddenness that few others can match. And this, too, is a fit metaphor for the still wobbly state of the Indian economy. Complacency about the eventual outcome would be dangerous. But to the artistry, charm, impulsiveness and passion that is the traditional heritage of Indian cricket, the new generation of players brings application, self-belief, tenacity and determination that rejects resigned acceptance of whatever fate has willed.

Recalling the ping-pong diplomacy that helped to normalize Sino-US relations, can relations between India and Pakistan be normalized with some courageous cricket diplomacy? Now that would be a fitting posthumous gift from the British Raj that left the subcontinent a deeply divided legacy in the first place.

30

India's nukes pose paradox for nonproliferation regime

The Japan Times, 14 March 2004

At the conclusion of their midlevel official talks in Islamabad on 16–18 February, India and Pakistan outlined an aggressive timetable for wide-ranging peace talks on Kashmir, nuclear safeguards, terrorism and other topics leading up to talks between the two foreign secretaries in May or June and between the foreign ministers in August. Negotiations will start in earnest after India's general elections tipped for late April and early May.

Meanwhile, US President George W. Bush's seven-point nonproliferation agenda got a cautious welcome from India. New Delhi agreed on the unsatisfactory state of the present nonproliferation regime, endorsed the principle of effective nonproliferation and called for consultations on the Bush initiative. But concrete cooperation will have to wait until some basic issues are clarified by Washington.

The international community is struggling to come to terms with the spate of recent revelations and confessions regarding proliferation activities by a number of countries that are signatories to the Nuclear Non-Proliferation Treaty (NPT). One difficulty is the status of the three countries outside the NPT that are known or believed to be de facto nuclear powers: Israel, Pakistan and India.

If the further spread of nuclear materials, skills and knowledge is to be halted completely, should these three countries be incorporated into existing and new regimes of restraint as partners, or should they be treated like pariahs with renewed, more strenuous efforts made to roll back their nuclear programs?

The dilemmas are best illustrated by considering the case of India. With regard to the Proliferation Security Initiative, which seeks to stop by force the clandestine trafficking in sensitive nuclear materials, New Delhi has so far maintained a studied silence. Given its long-standing complaints about the flow of material in its neighbourhood, India is sympathetic to the goals of PSI, but would want assurances about decision-making and the procedures to be followed for interdicting the traffic.

With the powerful Indian Navy sitting astride the Indian Ocean's sea lanes of communication, India's participation in the PSI would have military as well as political significance in broadening the base of this particular coalition of the willing.

Indian analysts insist that India's record on safeguarding its nuclear material is impeccable. They have been quick to point to the involvement of many European-based companies and individuals in Pakistani scientist Abdul Qadeer Khan's worldwide underground proliferation network. India's record on preventing proliferation is rather better than that of many European countries. Therefore, New Delhi should be comfortable with the call for a UN Security Council resolution to criminalize proliferation and require tight control over storage and exports of nuclear-sensitive material.

The call for a ban on selling enrichment and reprocessing equipment and technologies will not affect India as it already has a fully developed nuclear fuel cycle. And with a permanent seat on the Board of Governors of the International Atomic Energy Agency, India can cooperate with the call to reform the Agency.

From India's perspective, the tricky points in the Bush proposal concern the demand for dismantling weapons programs in problem countries and converting them to civilian research, and the requirement for signing the Additional Protocol to the NPT on tightened safeguards on national nuclear programs. That's because the points beg the question: Is India a problem country?

If Washington answers in the affirmative, no deal will be attractive enough to attract Indian interest. But in fact the whole thrust of US policy against the proliferation of weapons of mass destruction since 9/11 has shifted from universal to selective nonproliferation. Bush has famously declared that he would not permit the world's most destructive weapons to fall into the hands of the world's most dangerous regimes. Thus nuclear weapons in rogue hands are a problem, but not so in safe or good hands.

The nonproliferation regime is based on two critical assumptions: that the weapons themselves are the main threat and that states are equal in status, legitimacy and morality. Both assumptions are under serious challenge.

Are nuclear weapons in American and British hands really as dangerous to world peace as, for the sake of argument, they would be in Iraqi, Libyan and North Korean hands?

Washington has never made a fuss about Israel's nuclear status. If the world accepts India as a nuclear power, then that would allow New Delhi to come on board with respect to certain points in the Bush plan on the side of the nuclear haves.

For this to happen, the world will have to break the habit of bracketing India with Pakistan. Throughout the Cold War, India made the mistake of moral equivalence between Moscow and Washington. Indians argue that the West is now making the same mistake with India and Pakistan. Washington's three priority concerns are promoting democracy, preventing proliferation and defeating terrorism. India is not a problem country on any one of the three.

For years, India has complained about Pakistan's proliferation and terrorist links. Having dismissed these concerns as self-serving rhetoric, Washington has now bought Islamabad's line about rogue individuals engaged in cowboy deals for their own profit.

Former Pakistani Prime Minister Benazir Bhutto was quoted last month as saying: "It is simply not credible that Pakistan's leading nuclear scientist, A.Q. Khan, was acting on his own exporting nuclear technology abroad. He could not have done what he did without the generals, and probably President Pervez Musharraf himself, being involved."

Leaving Pakistan's culpability aside, how can India be accepted as a legitimate nuclear power without undermining the entire NPT regime, the world's most successful arms control agreement in history? And will others who have signed and honoured the NPT not feel betrayed if India is rewarded for its "bad" behaviour in 1998 – an example of what philosophers call "moral hazard"?

We do have a problem. If the international community tries to deal with India within the framework of nonproliferation, then, six years on from 1998, this is a very strange definition of realism on an issue of nuclear security. If the alternative framework of disarmament is used, then why insist on disarmament for just the three countries (India, Pakistan and Israel), and not all eight (the other five being Britain, China, France, Russia and the United States)?

Until this fundamental paradox is resolved, India cannot really decide on its response to the Bush initiative. But in addition to the global paradox, there is a local difficulty. If India demands and is conceded nuclear status by the world, while Pakistan is still treated as a problem country, what impact will this have on the embryonic peace process on the subcontinent?

31

The Iraq war in retrospect

The Japan Times, 28 March 2004

The question that crops up repeatedly when we register our opposition to the Iraq war is: would you rather then have Saddam Hussein still in power? It's a fair question that deserves a serious answer. Unlike in 1990, when Hussein did have a few admirers, last year he had none. This makes the failure of the American-British alliance to win any significant international support for the war all the more remarkable. It's not that we disliked the dictator less, but we disliked the war option even more.

Say I have a rat in my kitchen. I call in the exterminators. When they are finished, my crockery and glassware are shattered, my kitchen shelves and cupboards are broken, the food in my pantry is poisoned, and even my house is wrecked. If I complain about the cost being too high in relation to the removal of one rat, does that mean I like having a rat in the kitchen?

Hussein is gone, but let's look at the collateral wreckage:

First, the United Nations stands doubly damaged. Many say we failed the test of standing up to a tyrant who had brutalized his own people, terrorized his neighbours and thumbed his nose at the United Nations for 12 years. Many more say we failed to stand up to the United States in defence of a country that no longer threatened outsiders. As we are reminded on almost a daily basis, UN help could be quite useful now in repairing the damage because of its political legitimacy, moral authority and nation-building expertise. Those who wish to degrade the United Nations should be careful of what they wish.

Second, the relationship between the United Nations and the United

States is badly frayed. Yet they need each other, not just in Iraq, but also in Afghanistan, Haiti and elsewhere. Everyone in the United Nations recognizes the importance of the United States for the health of the international organization – but not at any cost. The credibility of the United Nations, its capacity to deliver on many US-supported and US-led goals are enhanced with the clear demonstration that on some issues of principle, the United Nations can say no to Washington. A completely pliant United Nations would indeed become irrelevant, even to the United States.

Third, trans-Atlantic relations have been damaged. Statements by the new Spanish prime minister have been quite robust about the need to re-align Spain with its natural friends and allies in Europe. When the major European nations said the case for war had not been proven beyond reasonable doubt, instead of dialogue they got bad-tempered insults. British support for Washington was so far removed from the dominant European sentiment that the British leader is in the last position to be helpful to Washington in gaining a respectful hearing in Europe.

Fourth, the fragile single European project has been badly shaken. The characterization of old and new Europe was in fact quite mistaken. Compared to the past few centuries of European history, France and Germany standing together in resisting war is the new Europe, built on peaceful relations embedded in continental institutions and the supremacy of the rule of law. And the former Soviet satellites that sided with the United States represent the continuity from the old Europe built on balance-of-power policies that had led to world wars.

Fifth, the United States has been deeply divided from world opinion. The latest cross-national public opinion polls continue to show plummeting confidence in US credibility and leadership. When two-thirds of Canadians – America's closest neighbours – believe that the US president lied his way into war, Washington does have a serious problem. Instead of shouting still more loudly, and in greater numbers, at an ungrateful world that has turned anti-American, Americans should pause, hold their breath and listen to others for a change. The major mainstream US news media could adopt a deliberate policy of exposing their American audiences to contrarian outside voices, instead of bombarding us with still more US points of view.

Sixth, the problem of US credibility with the Islamic world is more acute. Anecdotal evidence backs up poll after poll that Muslims are embittered and resentful of a perceived assault on Islam. Their sense of grievance is inflamed by perceptions of collective humiliation and rank double standards. The United States is so deeply unpopular that even pro-Western governments hesitate to speak in support of it these days.

Seventh, the US people are domestically divided with an edge to their opinions that is quite disheartening for all well-wishers of the country and those who recognize that the American role in world affairs as a virtuous great power has been historically unique, essentially beneficial and generous to a fault. The deep internal frictions are especially troubling because of the impressive national unity shown in the aftermath of the terror attacks on 11 September 2001.

Eighth, the precedent has been set for attacking another country on the basis of unilateral allegations and suspicions of a threat to national and international security. How are we going to prevent the proliferation of the unlawful and unjustified use of force, as an instrument of state policy, by other countries? Neither America nor anyone else needs a permission slip from the United Nations to defend itself. The UN Charter recognizes the right to self-defence. But the permission slip is required for another country to attack you, or for you to attack another country, other than in self-defence.

Ninth and finally, the net result of all this has been a distraction from the war on terror. The fall from grace of an America that was the object of everyone's sympathy and support after 9/11 is nothing short of astonishing. That support understood and backed the war against the Taliban government of Afghanistan. It fractured when Washington turned its attention to Iraq, whose links to 9/11 were tenuous at best.

Am I glad that Hussein is gone? You bet. There are other benefits as well. Rogue regimes of proliferators, torturers and mass murderers have been put on notice. Some like Libya have tried to pull back from the brink, though others like North Korea may have been spurred in the opposite direction. There is still the potential to remake the regional order in Iraq's neighbourhood.

The war has also given real urgency to the debates on reforming the system of multilateral governance so that we focus on real threats through collective efforts.

Was the war worth it? For Hussein's tribal supporters in the Tikrit region, no. For the minority Kurds and majority Shiites, yes. For the world as a whole? You be the judge.

32

New jailers, same prison?

The Japan Times, 15 May 2004

The stage-managed toppling of ex-Iraqi President Saddam Hussein's statue will not, after all, be the image defining the Iraq war. Like the famous photo of the young girl on fire running naked to escape the horror of napalm in the Vietnam War, the photographs emerging from Abu Ghraib prison will be the icons defining this most ill-advised and ill-planned war. They have managed to combine everything that is most depraved in victors by inflicting the worst possible humiliations and indignity in the Arab world: the grotesque pyramid of naked bodies in suggestive poses while soldiers ham it up for the camera; a woman guard with a naked prisoner on a leash; forcing men in hoods to kneel before the guards in the presence of their wives and children.

The inhuman cruelty is exceeded only by incompetence beyond belief. The conquerors have sunk to the same level of depravity as the thugs they sought to displace. Yet the reactions within America also point to the fallacy of imposing moral equivalence between Hussein's regime and the US administration.

It is worth making four arguments:
- The abuses are not isolated incidents, but reflect a systemic malaise.
- The abuses flow from the backdrop and manner of going to war.
- Also on display have been the self-correcting mechanisms of a great and enduring democracy.
- The need for a constructive cleanup of the Iraq mess is more urgent than ever.

In a public lecture last month (in Canberra), I said: "The implications of Guantanamo Bay (Cuba) are so revolutionary, so far-reaching and so frightening that they are worth underlining." In effect the United States asserted the right to be able to "pick up foreign citizens anywhere in the world, spirit them off to Guantanamo and lock them up forever, with no court questioning its actions" (David Cole, *The Nation*, 8 December 2003). The main purpose was to take the prisoners beyond the reach of any law that could protect them.

Moreover, emboldened by the curtailment of civil liberties in the bastion of democracy, many other governments have appropriated the language of the war on terror to wage their own wars on domestic dissidents. Now we learn of how Macedonia killed a group of Pakistani immigrants in cold blood in 2002 to impress upon Washington the sincerity of its commitment to the war on terror.

This is why Abu Ghraib is a logical and predictable outcome of the consistent and repeated pattern of abuses of human rights in violation of international conventions and norms, based on a cavalier dismissal of centuries-old legal principles to protect prisoners from abuse at the hands of captors and guards.

Over the last few years, hubris has grown as Washington became openly dismissive of many international regimes, including arms control, climate change and international criminal justice. When US Defense Secretary Donald Rumsfeld arrogates the right to determine unilaterally the status of captured people and their proper treatment, and then dismisses allegations of mistreatment and torture with "stuff happens"; when captives (many subsequently confirmed to be innocent) are handed over for interrogation to regimes where torture is known to be practised: Should ordinary soldiers be faulted for concluding that their prisoners – who must be guilty, otherwise they wouldn't be prisoners, right? – are subhuman scum unworthy of being treated like human beings?

Worse is to root this in the war itself. The restraints of international law on waging war were pushed aside as mere inconveniences. Soldiers were ordered to war on the basis of falsehoods, no matter how sincerely believed. They were asked not just to die, but to kill. The administration misled them and the public into identifying the Iraqi regime with "9/11," the thirst for vengeance for which is yet to be sated.

Should we be surprised if some soldiers square their conscience by concluding that the enemy is subhuman? How else to account for the killing of 300 to 600 Fallujahns, including many innocent women and children, in vengeance for four Americans who were killed and mutilated? When leaders exempt themselves from the norms of international behaviour, a few foot soldiers will free themselves from the norms of civilized conduct.

And yet. It is Americans who led the world in publishing the pictures, reacting to them as a society with revulsion and deep disgust, conducting an anguished debate in the opinion columns and shows, promising a due accounting and justice for the perpetrators, and issuing apologies from the president down. Were that other countries could match them in such swift and honest introspection. I hope the lights shining in the city on the hill – a powerful symbol for millions of us from and in developing countries whose significance sadly escapes too many Americans – are not extinguished in my lifetime, if ever.

In the meantime, we do have a mess on our hands. Iraqi transition, reconstruction and nation-building cannot be allowed to fail, not after everything that has happened. Genuine control and authority needs to be transferred to the United Nations, for surely the United States now has passed irretrievably into the enemy camp as far as Iraqis are concerned. The damage to US credibility and image in the Arab and Islamic world will take at least a generation to recover; Iraq's recovery must start now. Time for the surreal coalition of the willing to hand over charge to the real international community.

The whole sorry episode also underlines the urgent need for the International Criminal Court's jurisdiction to cover the international military actions of all countries without class distinctions based on wealth and power.

Absolute power corrupts absolutely. Those in charge of guarding prisoners amid an ongoing war need to establish and assert absolute control over captives. They do so under conditions of almost total secrecy. Because the psychological restraints of ordinary day-to-day living on the urge to sadistic behaviour begin to fall away, it is imperative that control systems be put in place to ensure that the actions and behaviour of captors conform to international conventions and humanitarian law. Otherwise there will indeed be moral equivalence between the bad and good guys, and they might as well put up a sign at the entrance saying "Open for business under new management."

33

Iraq needs better security, legitimacy, economy

The Daily Yomiuri, 15 June 2004

The Iraq war roiled the world of international diplomacy as few other issues have since 1945. Those waging war insisted that it was both legal and legitimate. Others conceded that it may have been illegal, but was still legitimate – an unflattering judgment on the adequacy of existing international law. A third group insisted it was both illegal and illegitimate.

Similarly, there were three views on the significance of the war for the UN-US relationship. US President George W. Bush famously declared that by refusing to support the war, the United Nations had rendered itself irrelevant. Others countered that the vigour and tenor of the worldwide debate showed how central the United Nations still is to the great issues of war and peace; the failure to obtain a UN authorization robbed the war of legitimacy and legality. A third group insisted that if the UN Security Council had been bribed and bullied into authorization, the United Nations would have been complicit in a war of aggression.

Now the United Nations and the United States have come together again with the unanimous adoption of Resolution 1546, which contains the seeds of conferring full-spectrum international respectability on Iraqi reconstruction. We all have a vital stake in stabilizing it, containing terrorism and moving beyond the Iraq mistakes.

The US Army is not suited to a quasi-imperial vision. Built for high-intensity warfare, it has difficulty engaging in peace operations and, once abroad, lacks both staying power and nation-building skills. By contrast, the United Nations has credibility and legitimacy in reintegration of former combatants, reconciliation of former enemies and reconstruction of war-torn societies.

After Abu Ghraib, the damage to US credibility and image in the Arab-Islamic world will take a generation to recover. Iraq's recovery must start now. The following is a sketch of the tasks requiring urgent attention in Iraq.

First, stabilizing the security situation. The current trends are in the wrong direction, with far too many kidnappings, attacks on and casualties among Iraqi officials and civilians, occupying forces and humanitarian agencies. The maintenance of law and order has displaced the building of a new Iraq as the top priority. The depressing spiral towards the breakdown of law and order has to be halted and reversed. Insurgents must be tracked down, contained, progressively constricted to narrower operating bases and eventually defeated. This may require readjustments in the force mix of military units and contributors, and a better balance between responding to provocations without alienating hearts and minds. Fallujah was an example of what not to do.

Security Council Resolution 1546 can provide the mandate for a new command structure. We also need appropriate force contributions from, for example, Arab and Islamic and other countries. France is lukewarm, saying the North Atlantic Treaty Organization's military participation would be neither timely nor well understood. Last year's European indignation is this year's apathy. But the Organization of Islamic Conference recently concluded a special meeting at which it called for greater contributions from members to a UN-controlled operation.

Second, the recovery of domestic, regional and international legitimacy. For all three, some form of constitutional recognition by the Security Council was always going to be necessary. The United Nations has had to tread the fine line between being seen as legitimizing an illegal and unjust war by collaborating with the occupiers, and abandoning the people of Iraq who are the true victims thrice over (of former Iraqi President Saddam Hussein's brutality, UN sanctions and the US war). Resolution 1546 endorses the formation by 30 June 2004 of an interim government, transparently a US creation with qualified sovereignty and time-limited legitimacy. A Transitional National Assembly is to be convened on the basis of direct elections by the end of 2004, if possible, or by the end of January 2005 otherwise, to draft a constitution under which a new government will be chosen by 31 December 2005.

The special representative of UN Secretary-General Kofi Annan will assist the political process. But Lakhdar Brahimi has publicly described Paul Bremer as the dictator who calls the shots in Iraq. Domestic legitimacy will be fully recovered only with the genuine transfer of power and return of confiscated sovereignty by the end of the process, not on 30 June.

Third, the reconstruction of Iraqi infrastructure. This cannot be done as a US monopoly, but requires much broader participation by members of the Arab, European and international community. Moreover, given the vast sums of money involved and the need to build, not lose, legitimacy, the international aid and reconstruction efforts must be managed transparently, without favouritism.

Finally, nation-building, state-building and economic development. Iraq's economic development has been retarded since Saddam's 1990 invasion of Kuwait and the sequence of events set in train by that. Its political development was arrested by the collapse of the state of Iraq into the personal fiefdom of Saddam. And its national welfare was conflated into the welfare of his clan.

For peace to be established in Iraq, we need simultaneously to pursue the goals of establishing and consolidating liberal democracy (meaning not just one-off elections, but representative institutions that hold elected governments accountable to the people and the rule of law, institutions of accountability like an independent judiciary and free press, guaranteed protection of minority rights embedded within majority rule, enforceable contracts and property rights), a thriving market economy to underpin economic growth and prosperity and a robust and resilient civil society to underwrite social and political stability.

34

On balance, charges do have some merit

The Canberra Times, 12 August 2004

The open letter from 43 former top Australian officials is without precedent in Australia, although it follows earlier British and American examples. It reflects the lifelong and continuing commitment to the security and welfare of Australia by some of the nation's most distinguished public servants.

The single most solemn and grave foreign policy responsibility of any government is to take the nation to war and ask its soldiers to kill others and risk their own lives. A government does so on the basis of its best assessments of the national interest.

In responding to the criticism, the government needs to be careful. Elections in Spain and Britain have already documented widespread and intense anger at perceptions by people of being misled by their own government. Much better to make a counter-case either justifying the original decision, or explaining it as an error with hindsight but one made in good faith. Rubbishing the age or impugning the motives of critics will prove counter-productive.

In world affairs governments rarely have the luxury of dealing with certainty, but must act on the balance of probability. Are the retired officials, acting with the full benefit of 20-20 hindsight, holding the government to too high a standard?

There would appear to be three main grounds for their attack on the government's Iraq policy: that it was based on falsehoods, that it has worsened the terrorist threat and that it has overly privileged the relationship with Washington at the cost of other important national interests.

The key to the first charge of course is the "demn'd elusive" weapons of mass destruction (WMD). The first point to note here is the near unanimous belief around the world that Saddam Hussein did have some WMD. For all we know, even Saddam himself may have believed this to the bitter end. The failure to find any cannot retrospectively invalidate this universal belief.

That said, the second, to me equally incontrovertible, contention is that almost all reasonable analysts and commentators – that is, all without an ideological predisposition to go to war against Iraq and find a plausible excuse to do so – agreed that Saddam's existing arsenal and programs did not constitute an imminent security threat. Even Colin Powell's and Condoleezza Rice's pre-9/11 statements show this. If there really were senior people within the intelligence community who believed otherwise then they should be sacked forthwith for gross incompetence.

The case for war therefore had to be more sophisticated. We know Saddam had them in the past, had no compunction about using them against Iran and his own people, was interested in re-acquiring them by hook or by crook, and would not hesitate to use them once he had them again. It would be far more challenging to confront him after he had his hands on usable WMD than before. Prudence required that he be pre-emptively disarmed the evening before, not the morning after.

The issue then becomes a matter of political judgment on whether Saddam was indeed the most serious WMD proliferation challenge, whether war was the only or the best weapon to end the threat and whether a war to oust him would reduce or exacerbate the challenge in other places. On this count the governments that chose to go to war are open to the charge of having made the wrong judgment call. All available evidence – governments can no more demand certainty of critics than the other way round: both are dealing with probability scenarios – seems to suggest that most regimes concluded that Saddam was attacked because he did not have usable WMD, North Korea has been spared because it might have such weapons. The policy conclusions of this are not reassuring for the rest of us.

Similarly with regard to terrorism. The comment that all the 43 officials retired before 11 September 2001 and so fail to appreciate how 9/11 changed the world runs away from the most serious charge of dereliction of duty. Not only has Iraq proven a distraction from the war on terror waged by the United States and its allies – and an enormous recruitment boon to the jihadists – both these are so obvious by now that arguing against merely enrages. The increased risk of being a target would have been an acceptable cost had in fact Iraq been complicit in 9/11.

Instead, the war shifted focus from those who were most responsible for 9/11. Like any good detective thriller, the price of the police being fixated on the wrong person is not simply convicting the innocent, but letting the true culprit get away. The real debate ought to have been why so many of the international terrorists of the 1990s had some connections to Saudi Arabia, Egypt and Pakistan (though not to the governments of these countries). These are supposed to be US allies. Can the war on terror be won without tackling this tough question? And why have the tough-minded journalists proven to be marshmallows in not pursuing this?

Which brings us to the final charge. Surely it is beyond question that the real reason for Australia going to war was because Washington so decided? Or that if the United States pulled out of Iraq tomorrow, so would Australia? The government was not pushing for this war, but followed America into it and will follow it out.

The alliance is of fundamental importance. Supporting the United States in its hour of military need is an honourable and defensible policy for any Australian government. But it can never be the only consideration, for that would subordinate national interests to US whim. Going along with US policy for the sake of getting along with Americans is a slogan, not a policy. We should fight alongside them if we believe this to be right, regardless of the level of unpopularity in the rest of the world. And we should refuse if we believe it to be wrong, regardless of the (temporary) unpopularity in Washington. North Atlantic Treaty Organization allies Canada, France and Germany sat out this war and have come out the better for it.

Joining the Americans in a wrong or unnecessary war, on the argument that it is obligatory because of the alliance, puts the survival of the alliance at risk. Similarly, sometimes force must be used to defend national or uphold international security. But the use of force recklessly, unwisely and hastily reduces the chances of it being used when really necessary.

35

Why we shouldn't rush to war over Darfur

The Globe and Mail, 11 September 2004

This week, the US administration applied the politically-loaded term "genocide" to the violence in Darfur, rhetoric that has raised the possibility of outside intervention to curb the rapes, murders and marauding that has driven hundreds of thousands of people from their homes in Sudan.

Who will save us from virtue run amok, from humanitarians clamouring for yet another war? Those who claim the moral high ground are disdainful of diplomats on the low road to compromise based on negotiations. In the realm of righteous cause and moral rectitude, principles are not for sale, values are not for bargaining.

Now the humanitarians' moral imperative is on the march again in Darfur. The tragedy is genuine, and the Sudanese regime may well be guilty of serial genocide over decades. Yet war is such a terrible calamity, with so much suffering and so much unpredictable, that it must always be the very last and rare option.

A Western intervention, far from offering a solution, may add to the problems. Especially after Iraq, we have to work with regional governments and through the United Nations.

The paucity of non-Western voices in the opinion pages of the dominant world media is striking. There seems to be little interest even in contemplating the possibility that developing countries might have some justice on their side in resisting assaults on sovereignty.

The most important clue to understanding their concerns is the history of Europe's encounter with Arabs, Africans and Asians.

The relentless march of colonialism and imperialism is never based on anything so vulgar as commercial and geopolitical calculations: land and wealth grabs. No, it is always driven by far loftier goals, such as spreading Christianity, or mentoring us in the virtues of democracy, human rights and the rule of law, or giving us peace.

They came to deliver us from local tyrants and stayed to rule as foreign despots. In the name of enlightenment, they defiled our lands, plundered our resources and expanded their empires. Some, like the rapacious Belgians in Congo, left only ruin, devastation and chaos whose dark shadows continue to blight. Others, like the British in India, left behind ideas, ideals and structures of good governance and the infrastructure of development alongside memories of national humiliation.

The record of Western colonizers as peacemakers is a sorry one, from Cyprus and Palestine to Congo, Zimbabwe, Sudan and South Asia. The legacy of smouldering sectarian conflicts and ethnic hatred should induce caution, diffidence and humility. Yet the past few years have been one of Britain's most war-prone periods since empire, rooted, remarkably, in an irresistible sense of moral mission.

Western colonialism explains why the fine talk of "humanitarian intervention" translates in our historical consciousness into efforts to resurrect and perpetuate rule by foreigners, why we are suspicious of military action guided by an enduring belief in being a virtuous power, and why we look for the ugly reality of geostrategic and commercial calculations camouflaged in lofty rhetoric.

Should we be mute accomplices when Westerners substitute their mythology of humanitarian intervention for our histories of colonial oppression? Do they think we do not remember, or do they simply not care?

If the major powers wish to help victims instead of helping themselves, they would do well to abandon the language of "humanitarian intervention" and embrace, instead, the vocabulary of the "responsibility to protect" as recommended by a broadly representative and independent international commission.

There is no question that we face a crisis of horrific proportions in Darfur, where 30,000 people have died and more than a million have been displaced. It is also beyond dispute that the government in Khartoum is, at worst, directly complicit for having encouraged, armed and aided the janjaweed militias in their orgy of atrocities in Darfur; at best, it bears indirect culpability for lacking the will or capacity to halt the atrocities.

But given the history of past interventions by Westerners, wiser counsel should prevail, and the African Union or the United Nations – which has been trying for more than a year to alert everyone to the gravity of the Darfur crisis – must accept the lead responsibility. If London and Washington lead the charge to eliminate the veto power in the Security

Council, then – but only then – can they claim legitimacy for military intervention outside the UN framework if UN authorization is vetoed.

There have been suggestions from some, such as *The Economist*, that Beijing and Moscow might tacitly accept Western intervention rather than set the precedent of authorizing UN intervention.

This is specious and self-serving. A history and pattern of interventions unauthorized by the Security Council creates new law in its wake, progressively legalizing such habitual state practice, without the compensating benefit of shared control over the policy through the United Nations. Why would Beijing and Moscow want to be party to such a self-defeating subterfuge?

The African Union, with 53 UN members, was created to provide African solutions to Africa's problems. The Darfur crisis is an excellent opportunity for Africans to take collective action, with the encouragement and assistance of outsiders. If developing countries wish to end interference by outsiders, they must assume the burden of responsibility for ending atrocities by one of their own. A good example along these lines is East Timor, where the lead was taken by the regional community (including Australia and New Zealand) with UN backing.

Given the size of the region (Sudan, Africa's largest country, is as big as Western Europe), the complex historical roots of the current crisis that cloud the moral clarity on which military action on perpetrators against victims has to be based, and the ease with which Western intervention could be exploited as yet another assault on Arabs and Muslims, the prospects for a successful outcome of the use of unilateral military force are questionable.

Those impatient for war against Sudan should also answer other critical questions. If deadlines are set by outsiders, does this not reduce rebels' incentives to negotiate an end to the conflict? How do they propose to address the moral hazard of encouraging all rebel groups to internationalize their crises by intensifying violence? Do developing countries not have the right to use force to put down armed challenge to their authority? Who decides the answers to these questions other than regional countries and the United Nations?

36

Not so brave new world: Three years after 9/11, and the world still lives in fear of terrorism

The Canberra Times, 11 September 2004

"9/11" was a split-screen moment that marked the end of the post-Cold War world and defined the new age of post-modern terror.

Evil beyond imagination, it destroyed forever the comforting myth of the invulnerability of the American homeland to nomadic enemies from distant lands engaged in far-off quarrels. We all watched in growing horror, grieved as one with the United States, and shared and understood its pain, anger and thirst for vengeance. The loss of innocence and disbelief at "crime beyond guilt" was reprised in recent days in the slaughter of the lambs in Beslan, Russia.

Australians, too, have shared in the trauma. Almost half the 202 lives lost in the Bali bombings of October 2002 were Australian. Again this week, when on Thursday a terrorist attack on the Australian Embassy in Jakarta captured the nation's attention, it highlighted our vulnerability in this new, threatened world order.

The first set of consequences of 9/11 was the rallying of Americans and uniting the world behind America; shaking Americans from the torpor of the Cold War victory and concentrating minds on the new threats to security. The promptness and decisiveness of Washington's response won the support and admiration of all. The subsequent rush into the blind alley of Iraq caused the United States to lose focus in the war on terrorism, squander the enormous goodwill of the world, divide America from friends old and new, weaken existing structures of cooperation across the Atlantic, sideline the United Nations as the arena for global cooperation, jeopardize the civil liberties of many people, and polarize America.

Terrorism is as old as human history. Osama bin Laden's evil genius was to fuse the fervour of religious schools, the rallying power of the call to holy war (jihad), the cult of martyrdom through suicide, the reach of modern technology, and the march of globalization into the new phenomenon of global terrorism. From Madrid to Beslan and Jakarta, the confetti of global terrorism is an ever present reminder that we are no safer than three years ago. In the immediate aftermath, the Bush administration did a superb job of staying calm, reassuring a traumatized and jittery nation, acting with deliberation instead of in haste, and rallying world support behind the plan to destroy the Taliban and al-Qaeda. The horror of the atrocity also forced many Muslims to confront the need to exorcise fundamentalist extremism from their midst.

The longer-term effects of 9/11 include a critical questioning of the Westphalian fiction of a world order based on sovereign states equal in status, legitimacy and power. In the real world they are anything but. Some are states only in name, with no capacity to make and enforce rules; others are ruled by criminal thugs; still others are foreign stooges. The deadly effectiveness of a handful of people using a combination of box cutters as weapons and commercial planes and their own bodies as missiles forced a fundamental re-think. Major security threats now come as much from failing states outside the Westphalian system as from strong states within.

This led to warnings of the risk of the world's most destructive weapons falling into the hands of the world's most dangerous rogues. That is, weapons in themselves are less of a threat than their possession by rogue actors. Moreover, treaty-based regimes may no longer offer adequate security, or may not have the capacity to enforce timely compliance. Hence the need to take precautions ahead of time, to stop the threats before they materialize through preemptive and preventive action.

In turn this calls into question the existing architecture of world order, as recognized by United Nations Secretary-General Kofi Annan who gathered together a high-level panel to advise him on what might be done to preserve the United Nations as the forum of choice for managing global threats.

But then US policy was hijacked by the neoconservatives to pursue their own, pre-9/11 agenda – the net effect of which has been damage to US interests and image. Saddam Hussein had been in their cross-hairs since his survival in Gulf War I. For reasons that remain clouded, the United States decided on attacking Iraq and ousting Saddam long before the job was done in Afghanistan of eradicating all remnants of the Taliban and securing the rule of the new regime. 9/11 provided a convenient alibi.

Impressions were deliberately fostered of Saddam's complicity in the attacks, fears were raised about weapons of mass destruction and a crisis requiring war was fabricated where none existed.

The United Nations, it can be safely said now, had done an excellent job of disarming Saddam after 1991. Bush went to the United Nations not to praise it but to bury it when it refused to authorize an unnecessary war. A self-righteous administration, convinced of its moral rectitude, disrespectful of advice, dismissive of criticism, and confident of its might, turned the full ferocity of its attention to Iraq. The victory on the battlefield was as brilliant as it has turned out to be pyrrhic.

Hubris had blinded the Pentagon to the need to plan for the day after. Contempt for the State Department as the source of endless nuancing – paralysis through analysis – meant that it was kept outside the loop. Arabists, brushed aside as captive of their subject, had warned of the anti-US nationalist fervour that would sweep Iraq and the Muslim world if liberation turned into occupation.

Now more than 1,000 American soldiers have died because some lied, and there is a rising tide of hostility to US policies around the world. The values of human rights and civil liberties that the United States championed for decades have taken a beating.

The dismissal of plummeting US prestige and credibility as anti-Americanism is wrong. But the many self-correcting mechanisms of US democracy, from the judiciary and press to civil society, have begun to reassert themselves to restore the balance between national security and civil liberty. As founding father Benjamin Franklin had warned, those who sacrifice essential liberty to temporary safety deserve neither.

The damage done to the war on terrorism will be harder to reverse. Judged by results and not rhetorical bombast, al-Qaeda's strategic blunder of 9/11 has been offset by the fallout from Iraq as Osama bin Laden became Osama bin Forgotten. Muslims who had empathized with the United States after 9/11 are more strongly alienated from Washington than ever before, fearful of an all-out assault on Islam. Talk of promoting democracy and the rule of law is belied not just by the events in Iraq, but also by the choice of allies in Central Asia and elsewhere which makes a mockery of claims that the United States has learnt from past mistakes of expedient relations with tyrants in power at the expense of fostering good governance based on the consent of the people.

Most importantly, in the insistence on "decontextualizing" terrorism so that no grievance or cause can possibly be seen as justifying it, Washington lost sight of the dual need to be tough on terrorists and tough on the causes of terrorism. In calls to condemn and kill terrorists in the name of moral clarity, the balance between short-term military measures and long-term political remedies was lost.

We have learnt to live with greater vigilance by law enforcement agencies and more intrusive security procedures for air travel, sometimes to the point of outright silliness. In tackling today's priorities in the "war on terrorism," there is a tension between identifying, apprehending, trying and punishing the terrorists and adopting a holistic approach for "draining the swamp of terrorism." It means stiffening the capacity and determination of governments to hunt down killers. But it also means strengthening institutional capacity to uproot the last remnants of terrorist infrastructure in countries in which terrorist cells are located, and ameliorating the conditions and grievances that motivate people to support and become terrorists.

37

Choosing how to intervene

The Japan Times, 10 October 2004

From Iraq to Darfur, the topic of international intervention to protect people from the brutality of their own governments remains a deeply divisive one for the international community. Western countries are likely to be the subjects not objects of intervention, and their worldview is coloured by this simple fact. Developing countries are seen as being bitterly opposed to such interventions.

Yet in extensive consultations across the world, the International Commission on Intervention and State Sovereignty (ICISS) found a surprising degree of agreement among developing countries that belies the rhetoric of rejectionism.

On the one hand, there is general acknowledgment of a disturbing vacuum in our collective humanitarian system to cope effectively with massacres and other tragedies. On the other hand, the attachment to sovereignty is rooted in painful historical encounters, and many have understandable fears that generalizing a supposed right to intervention could be abused by the great powers to launch unilateral interventions.

At the same time, it is just as important that leaders of the South examine their own policies and strategies critically. Instead of forever opposing, complaining and finding themselves on the losing side anyway, developing countries must assume the burden of responsibility for ending atrocities by one of their own. Otherwise they risk simply being dismissed as the international "nattering nabobs of negativism."

Nowhere did we encounter an absolute rejection of intervention. In all consultations, people were prepared to concede that, sometimes, outsiders may indeed have to step in with military force to protect innocent victims from perpetrators of mass killings and ethnic cleansing.

Most interlocutors expressed reservations regarding the term "humanitarian," saying it should never be associated with war. The weight of historical baggage is too strong for a new consensus to be formed around the concept of "humanitarian intervention."

In all our consultations, people emphasized the central importance of the United Nations. The organization, the only authentic representative of the international community, embodies the existing international moral code and political consensus on the proper rules of conduct. If the code and consensus have become obsolete, then the United Nations is still the only proper forum and arena for renegotiating the terms of engagement of individual states with a single international standard of civilization.

Any one intervention does not simply violate the sovereignty of any given target state in any one instance; it also challenges the principle of a society of states resting on a system of well-understood and habitually obeyed rules. If the United Nations is unequal to the international responsibility to protect, then it must be reformed.

Neither Britain nor the United States has ever indicated that the elimination of the veto clause would be acceptable to them. That being the case, developing countries can be forgiven for concluding that calls for a derogation of sovereignty whenever coalitions of the willing so decide is simply yet another power grab, based on the negotiating adage that what we have is ours, what you have is open to negotiation. In fact the point was made repeatedly and everywhere that if the Security Council is going to be more assertive in authorizing military interventions, then it will fail the test of legitimacy without a major reform of the composition and procedures of the Council.

There is unanimous opposition to the idea of Western military interventions unauthorized by the United Nations. There is far too much historical baggage for suspicions and fears to be allayed simply on assurances of good faith and intention. And yet, paradoxically, there is reluctance to rule out the idea that sometimes some individual or groups of states may have to take military action in the face of a paralyzed United Nations.

All parts of the developing world (as well as others) are seriously concerned with issues of double standards and selectivity. Developing countries are united in the insistence that external intervention must never lead to territorial breakup. Protection of at-risk peoples must not lead to new political or territorial arrangements imposed by external actors.

All this suggests that a new consensus on the tension between intervention and sovereignty is possible. But if we are going to get a new consensus, then the bar for intervention has to be set quite high, the circumstances legitimizing it have to be narrow and the procedural and operational safeguards to prevent abuse of the more permissive scope have to be tight:

- Interventions cannot become the pretext for imposing external political preferences with regard to regimes and political and economic systems. Cases justifying such action must be tightly restricted to such heinous crimes as genocide and mass murders
- Intervention must always be the last resort, and intervening forces must withdraw as soon as possible
- The actions of intervening forces inside the target country must be guided by considerations of political impartiality and neutrality between the domestic political contenders as well as strict fidelity to international humanitarian law
- Above all, intervening forces must respect and ensure the territorial integrity of the target state

38

Did Kosovo illuminate Iraq?

The Japan Times, 17 October 2004

One of the curious features of the Iraq war last year was the serious split across the Atlantic. And what seemed to puzzle as much as infuriate Americans was why the major European powers, having signed on to war without UN authorization in 1999 against Slobodan Milosevic, "the butcher of Belgrade," refused to do so in 2003 against Saddam Hussein, "the butcher of Baghdad."

On balance, the Americans would appear to have just cause for their complaint of double standards. To be sure, there are important differences. But in some respects the differences are exaggerated and, in other respects, important similarities overshadow the differences.

In 1999, on the one hand, there was compelling television footage of the humanitarian tragedy in Kosovo that outraged an internationalized human conscience. But just as the claims of weapons of mass destruction have been shown to have been greatly exaggerated and amplified through a surprisingly gullible media, so were the claims of mass murders of up to 200,000 people in Kosovo.

On the other hand, there was every prospect of prompt and effective military action being vetoed in the UN Security Council. So the North Atlantic Treaty Organization (NATO) launched a "humanitarian war" – a war over values, not interests – without UN authorization.

"Humanitarianism" was thus married to "war" in a clever and successful ploy that labelled opponents of the war as anti-humanitarian. Few noticed that the intervention was confined to bombing, leading to the logically absurd "humanitarian bombing."

The justification for a regional organization bypassing the international organization to wage an offensive war was as problematic then as last year. The Kosovo precedent remains deeply troubling for having posed a fundamental challenge to the normative architecture of world order.

The Independent International Commission on Kosovo concluded that NATO's intervention was illegal but legitimate. The intervention was illegal because the use of force is prohibited by the UN Charter except in self-defence or when authorized by the Security Council.

The intervention was legitimate, nevertheless, because of the scale of human rights atrocities by the Milosevic regime, the failure of other means used to try to stop those atrocities and the political stalemate in the Security Council created by Russia and China. Proponents of this argument clearly believe that legitimacy is on a higher plane than legality. Thus opposition to the perfectly legal apartheid regime in South Africa was fully justified: illegal, but legitimate.

There is a problem, nevertheless. Suppose I have witnessed a murder by a rich celebrity. Suppose further that, for reasons having to do with expensive trial lawyers who exploit every technicality, the murderer is acquitted. Can I claim legitimacy in inflicting vigilante justice on the murderer on the grounds that society is better off without him?

A normative commitment to the rule of law implies a commitment to the principle of relations being governed by law, not power. It also implies a willingness to accept the limitations and constraints of working within the law in specific instances of an illegitimate outcome.

The UN Security Council, as the core international law-enforcement system, has a monopoly on the legitimate use of coercive measures in international affairs. The best that can be said of the NATO actions was that they fell into "gray area" between lawfulness and legitimacy, where the use of force is neither condemned nor condoned, but tolerated.

Critics argued that NATO acted illegally in terms of its own constitution, the UN Charter and state practice. Supporters turned the normal process of reasoning upside down. The war was illegal, yet necessary and justified. Therefore the war highlighted defects in international law, not shortcomings in NATO action. The (anticipated) failure of the Security Council to authorize the war was a reflection on flaws in the Council's functioning, not on the invalidity of NATO bombing. The moral urgency underpinning NATO's actions, and the military success of those actions, would in due course shape legal justification to match the course of action.

In Kosovo, in 1999, a draft resolution to condemn NATO bombing was defeated 3–12, despite two permanent Council members voting for it. Many interpreted the failure to flash the red light as tacit authorization.

Therefore NATO neither flouted international legitimacy nor challenged Security Council authority. Rather, the Security Council failed to meet the challenge of international moral authority.

Put like this, the essential structural continuity from Kosovo in 1999 to Iraq in 2003 is at once apparent. For this was precisely the challenge posed to the United Nations by London and Washington: act to enforce your own resolutions and your own authority, or suffer a decline in your authority and become irrelevant.

It could be argued that the case against Iraq was not framed in terms of the humanitarian argument, but in terms of weapons of mass destruction, which have fallen apart completely.

True, but the case against Serbia in 1999 was not framed in humanitarian language either. People overlooked then that NATO's case was equally dubious. They went to war because Milosevic rejected the Rambouillet ultimatum. Had the Rambouillet diktat been given as close a scrutiny in 1999 as the WMD argument in 2003, it would likely have met with matching scepticism.

NATO succeeded in 1999 in diverting attention from Rambouillet to the humanitarian liberation argument. British Prime Minister Tony Blair and US President George W. Bush have had more difficulty trying to shift the chief justification from WMD to humanitarian outcomes in the case of Iraq.

The differences were that the ethnic cleansing by Milosevic was much closer in time to the 1999 war, not 15 years in the past. No NATO power had been complicit through diplomatic and material assistance to Serbia in the perpetration of those atrocities at the time that they were committed. The European powers collectively were simply sick and tired of Milosevic's deceit, evasions and atrocities being committed in Europe itself.

The Rambouillet diktat reflected the trans-Atlantic horror at Milosevic's record, and there was no oil that could be pointed to as the main motive for intervention. The humanitarian motive stood out far more clearly as the main driver of the intervention for most countries that went to war. Because of this, the major Western allies stood solidly united at the level of both people and governments in 1999, whereas the democratic alliance was deeply fractured last year.

Hussein's alleged links to international terrorism and al-Qaeda have also turned out to be based on deceptions and flawed conclusions drawn from heavily qualified, faith-based intelligence. Instead of policy being influenced by intelligence, a predetermined policy shaped the collection, analysis and interpretation of intelligence.

In the case of Serbia, one wonders how much closer scrutiny would have been given by NATO to the links between al-Qaeda and Serbia's main military opponents in Kosovo, the Kosovo Liberation Army, after 9/11?

The majority of developing countries were strongly opposed to the NATO intervention in Kosovo at the time. Their strongest opposition was grounded in the violation of the norm of nonintervention without UN authorization. Most NATO countries insisted that their action did not set a precedent. The Iraq war proves that claim to have been false.

In world affairs we do not have the luxury of "cherry-picking" parts of international law and norms. International do-gooders, like their domestic counterparts, must accept responsibility for the unintended but predictable consequences of their actions.

For nongovernmental organizations, countries and international groups, including both NATO and the United Nations, choices today have consequences on the morrow.

39

Cheerleaders for war round on the UN

The Canberra Times, 14 December 2004

As if the United Nations was not in enough difficulty already, it is embroiled in the biggest financial scandal of its history.

The failure by the secretary-general's son to come clean early and fully about the payment of non-compete fees from the Swiss firm under investigation has compounded perceptions of a conflict of interest, despite any evidence to suggest that Kofi Annan himself bears any complicity. The floundering efforts at explanation and justification indicate a lack of skill in modern public diplomacy that is a legacy of risk-aversion and publicity-shyness that have passed their use-by date.

One would think that the cheerleaders for waging war on Saddam Hussein's Iraq, on the thoroughly discredited grounds of weapons of mass destruction, would have retreated into a period of quiet introspection. In fact it is as difficult to find any trace of embarrassment, humility or repentance as to find a trace of the supposedly ubiquitous and deadly weapons of mass destruction in Iraq. Instead many of those columnists and newspapers, clearly believing that attack is the best form of defence, have gone on the offensive against the United Nations and against Secretary-General Kofi Annan personally.

And when Annan dared to caution against a major military offensive in Fallujah because of the heightened risk of civilian casualties, *The Wall Street Journal* in an editorial described the secretary-general's letter as "a hostile act" (8 November): not just wrong, not an error of judgment or a difference of interpretation, but an act of hostility towards the United States.

The fiercest attack on the United Nations has concentrated on the oil-for-food scandal.

Thus William Safire, writing in his *New York Times* column on 15 November, accused Annan of "stonewalling" and "obstruction of justice."

Demands for Annan's resignation have received wide US and international publicity. One could argue that such statements are consistent with the faith-based approach to intelligence and war that shaped policy prescriptions in the first place: (1) allegations=proof=conviction; (2) facts to the contrary can simply be brazened out through repeated denials; and (3) the law can be disregarded if it comes in the way.

Two separate scandals have been rolled into one: smuggling and bill padding.

The responsibility for preventing oil smuggling by Iraq lay with a maritime task force which included US Navy ships; the United Nations had no role in this. The General Accounting Office of the US Congress concluded that the maritime task force interdicted only 25 percent of the oil flow.

The Iraqis were also driving trucks to Turkey, Syria and Jordan. The United States and Britain, not the United Nations, had planes in the air to keep watch.

Then there is the matter of inflating the dollar figures in order to blacken the United Nations' image as much as possible. The total of all "illicit" revenue from 1996 to 2003 was originally estimated to be $10–11 billion. (If this is taken back to 1991, five years before the oil-for-food program began, the figure rises to $21 billion.) Of this, less than one-third was in the form of surcharges on oil sales and kickbacks on humanitarian imports.

The "scam" consisted of under-pricing Iraqi oil and overpricing goods purchased in return. Middlemen colluding in the twin scheme were bribed and the regime kept most of the price differentials in both sets of transactions.

UN overseers in the Office of the Iraq Programme raised concerns about price discrepancies and oil sales surcharges to the sanctions committee comprising all 15 members of the Security Council. The sanctions committee (not UN bureaucrats) decided whether or not to approve contracts. In the 18 months before the Iraq war, UN officials presented it with 70 contracts that were potentially overpriced. Not a single one of these was put on hold, not one.

The United States and Britain acted on concerns raised by UN officials and put on hold thousands of contracts. These related mainly to concerns about dual-use technologies, not price padding, bribes and kickbacks.

Not one of the 36,000 contracts was ever cancelled. Yet the whole scandal is being dumped solely on the United Nations.

Professor John Ruggie of Harvard University (former strategic adviser to Annan) suggests (*The International Herald Tribune*, 8 December 2004) that the US Congress should launch as rigorous and thorough an investigation of the role of US officials and companies (Halliburton, Ingersoll-Rand, General Electric) in ignoring Saddam Hussein's illicit activities as Annan has asked for with regard to the role of UN officials.

The sanctions committee reflected the competing priorities of the Security Council, especially the United States and Britain. Their top concerns were to disarm Saddam Hussein, starve him of resources to rearm in future, and minimize the collateral harm to his people caused by his policies. All three goals were largely achieved.

We can confidently assert now that Saddam was successfully disarmed by the United Nations. Over the life of the oil-for-food program (1996–2003), a basic food ration was provided for the 27 million Iraqis, the average daily intake of calories jumped by 83 percent, child malnutrition was halved (it has almost doubled again since the Iraq war last year) and the mortality rate of children under five plummeted.

After the scandal broke, Annan acted with alacrity. He sought full and immediate action by the Security Council and appointed people of impeccable integrity to conduct a thorough investigation, chaired by former US Federal Reserve Chairman Paul Volcker.

Safire writes of "the secretary-general's manipulative abuse of Paul Volcker" who cannot see how his integrity "is being shredded by a web of sticky-fingered officials and see-no-evil bureaucrats desperate to protect the man on top who hired him to substitute for and thereby to abort prompt and truly independent investigation" (*The New York Times*, 15 November 2004).

Whoa!

Annan has committed himself to full cooperation with the panel in providing all necessary documents and records, requiring UN officials to cooperate with it and making its report public. Understandably, some US Congressmen are unhappy that UN officials cannot be subpoenaed by the Volcker committee. But the United Nations does not have subpoena power to pass on to the committee. Yet Annan has ordered all UN staff to cooperate with the inquiry, on pain of dismissal. If the committee finds evidence of wrongdoing by UN staff, they can be pursued in national courts with the right to subpoena. And Annan has said publicly that UN officials will not be permitted to hide behind claims of diplomatic immunity.

In today's topsy-turvy world, this is stonewalling and obstruction of justice.

40

Rhetoric vs. the record: Freedom, when it suits US

The Japan Times, 12 February 2005

No one who watched the exhilaration and exuberance of Iraqis facing down the threat of bullets in order to cast their ballots can fail to have been moved. And for those who were actually in Iraq to witness this first-hand, battle-hardened and cynical journalists included, it must have been bliss indeed to be alive at dawn on 30 January and relief to be still alive at dusk. Ironically, the enthusiasm and courage with which ordinary people seized their opportunity to choose their own leaders is a repudiation of central parts of American foreign policy.

It is also a paradoxical explanation for the intensity of much anti-American sentiment. For it is a forceful reminder of just how strong the passion for freedom is, how strong the loathing for regimes and rulers who brutalize their own people is, and how bitter the feelings are towards outside powers who prefer to prop up friendly dictators rather than team up to topple them. The balance sheet of American support for, and opposition to, dictatorships has usually been negative for any given year since the end of World War II.

In pursuing such short-term tactics, US governments have betrayed not just the people yearning to overthrow their local tyrants, but also their own ideals. Many Americans fail to grasp the power of the metaphor of the shining lights of the city on the hill, the hypnotic pull of the ringing American declaration of independence, the stirring inspiration of President Abraham Lincoln's Gettysburg Address (1863). These are not just American treasures; they are the common heritage of mankind.

For India, the speech that most closely matches Gettysburg is Prime

Minister Jawaharlal Nehru's address to the nation on 14 August 1947, when the country became independent. At the stroke of midnight, when the world slept, he proclaimed an ancient nation awoke to freedom, keeping its tryst with destiny. The same festive atmosphere marked South Africa's liberation from apartheid; the same carnival-like celebration of freedoms has accompanied the holding of popular elections following the fall of every dictator of left and right.

Yet it is difficult to recall instances when, faced with a choice between a people rising in revolt and an oppressive but US-friendly regime, Washington actually sided with the people. The world today would have been poorer and sadder for many people if America had not helped to bring about an end to their tormentors, from Poland to Georgia and Ukraine. Nor can Washington fairly be asked to assume the burden of changing history for the better in all places all alone.

But the world is also poorer and sadder for many people because Washington so often compromised its ideals for the sake of stable relations with undemocratic regimes. Their people, including Mideast Arabs and Muslims, seek exactly what Americans take for granted: political freedoms, civil liberties, material prosperity, the right to hold on to legitimately acquired property and wealth, and the accountability of rulers to the rule of law. They are bewildered and embittered when Washington turns its face away from them so as not to antagonize friendly regimes or important allies.

The gap between the lofty, soaring rhetoric of liberty (mentioned 15 times) and freedom (27 times) in US President George W. Bush's second inaugural speech on 20 January and the reality of his administration's ties to authoritarian regimes is pronounced. In an especially eloquent passage, the president said:

> We have seen our vulnerability – and we have seen its deepest source. For as long as whole regions of the world simmer in resentment and tyranny – prone to ideologies that feed hatred and excuse murder – violence will gather, and multiply in destructive power, and cross the most defended borders, and raise a mortal threat. There is only one force of history that can break the reign of hatred and resentment, and expose the pretensions of tyrants, and reward the hopes of the decent and tolerant, and that is the force of human freedom.

Just so. And yet the passage is at odds with the actual record of the administration in its first term.

Similarly, in the light of the known treatment of prisoners in US military custody from Afghanistan and Guantanamo to Iraq, what is one to make of the president's boast that "from the day of our Founding, we have proclaimed that every man and woman on this earth has rights, and dignity, and matchless value, because they bear the image of the Maker of Heaven and Earth"? Or that "freedom, by its nature, must be sustained by the rule of law"?

And dare Palestinians put faith in the promise that "We will persistently clarify the choice before every ruler and every nation: The moral choice between oppression, which is always wrong, and freedom, which is eternally right"?

If all this marks an implicit acknowledgment of mistakes made in the first and a promise to do better in the second four years, then US precepts and practice may yet converge.

The United Nations too has been guilty of compromising core values, perhaps even more so than the United States. On some issues like racial equality and apartheid, the United Nations was well ahead of Washington in leading the good international fight. But overall, no objective historian of the past 60 years could credibly claim that victory in the great battles for defeating the evil of communism, or promoting the onward march of human rights and freedoms, was won by the world body rather than America.

In 1993, the people of Cambodia were given the chance to vote under UN supervision. Like terrorists in Iraq this year, the dreaded and barbaric Khmer Rouge tried to intimidate the people against voting. Instead the Cambodians showed great courage in voting in large numbers under UN-supervised elections. There is an argument to be made that the United Nations connived in negating the verdict at the polls because of the dominant power of the ruling regime in Cambodia, betrayed the people and undermined whatever prospect the tiny nation might have had for a democratic future within a foreseeable timeframe.

Moral clarity and backbone, essential for courage of convictions, do not sit easily alongside institutional timidity and instinctive risk-aversion. But for the international organization as for the sole superpower, there is a price to be paid in the long run for expedient decisions in the short term.

41

Intervention based on rules

The Japan Times, 10 April 2005

According to the UN High-Level Panel on Threats, Challenges and Change, "The maintenance of world peace and security depends importantly on there being a common global understanding, and acceptance, of when the application of force is both legal and legitimate."

The provision of security imposes two requirements. Those not authorized to use force should renounce its use and threat in their social relations, while the authorized agents of any community with the monopoly on the legitimate use of violence must have the capacity and will to use force when required.

For it to be efficient, any international enforcement action must be legitimate – in conformity with international law and consistent with the UN Charter. For it to be effective, it must match action to resources and be based on a unity of purpose and action in the international community and avoid fracturing the existing consensus. For it to be equitable, it must reconcile or, at the very least, balance competing interests among the many constituencies that make up the international community and avoid favouring the interests and viewpoints of one over the others.

To achieve freedom from fear, citizens must be assured that national authorities with the legal monopoly on the means of violence will not unleash the agents and instruments of violence on the people. Likewise, states must be assured that the most powerful will aim to settle differences of opinion around the negotiating table and not at the point of tank turrets, helicopter gunships and missiles.

Behind the headlines on the deeply divisive Iraq war was the larger question of the changing nature of threats in the modern world, the inadequacy of existing norms and laws in addressing them, and thus the need for new "rules of the game."

Intervention by the North Atlantic Treaty Organization in Kosovo in 1999 highlighted a triple-policy dilemma of complicity, paralysis and illegality. To respect sovereignty all the time is to risk being complicit in humanitarian tragedies sometimes. To argue that the UN Security Council must consent to international intervention for humanitarian purposes is to risk policy paralysis by handing over the agenda either to the passivity and apathy of the Council as a whole, or to the most obstructionist member of the Council, including any one of the five permanent members determined to use the veto clause. To use force without UN authorization is to violate international law and undermine world order.

The growing risks of a separation between lawfulness and legitimacy in the use of force, both domestically and internationally, can be attenuated through awareness of the responsibility to protect. The use of force, both domestically and internationally, must be tamed and brought under the restraining discipline of the rule of law.

Significant gaps exist in the legal and institutional framework to combat today's real threats. If international institutions cannot cope with them, states will do so themselves.

Given the changing nature of armed conflict, the need for clarity, consistency and reliability in the use of armed force for civilian protection now lies at the heart of the United Nations' credibility. Absent a new consensus and clarity, its performance will be measured against contradictory standards – exposing it to charges of ineffectiveness from some and irrelevance from others, increasing the probability of unauthorized interventions, and further eroding the Security Council's primacy as the protector of peace and security.

The International Commission on Intervention and State Sovereignty published its landmark report "The Responsibility to Protect" (R2P) with exceptionally bad timing in December 2001. The world was preoccupied with the war on terror. But R2P has gained currency in the meantime. Its main conclusions find their way into the High-Level Panel's report, including five criteria for legitimacy: seriousness of threat, proper purpose, last resort, proportional means and balance of consequences.

During ICISS worldwide consultations, I was struck by four facts:

- A strong consensus that sovereignty is not an absolute barrier to international intervention when exercising the responsibility to protect
- An equally strong consensus that Security Council authorization for intervention is preferable to all other alternatives
- Insistence by very few that Council authorization is necessary in all cases

- Considerable concern to avoid discrediting the United Nations or undermining respect for an international order based on rules and law rather than on power and wealth

Our ability to act beyond our borders, even in the most distant spots, have increased tremendously. This has produced a corresponding increase in demands and expectations "to do something."

The concept of the responsibility to protect removes the last remaining excuses for us to sit back and do nothing when confronted with atrocities. In the real world today, our choice is not between intervention and nonintervention, but between ad hoc and rules-based intervention – unilateral vs. multilateral.

The challenge is neither to deny the reality of intervention nor to denounce it, but to manage it for the better. Establishing agreed principles to guide the use of force will make it more difficult to appropriate the humanitarian label to self-serving interventions, while making the Security Council more responsive to the security needs of civilians.

In his 21 March report, UN Secretary-General Kofi Annan urged the Council to adopt a resolution "setting out these principles and expressing its intention to be guided by them" when authorizing the use of force. This would "add transparency to its deliberations and make its decisions more likely to be respected, by both governments and world public opinion."

All too often, such statements from the United Nations today arouse cynicism among commentators. But we should remember one important fact: 15 years is a very short time in the sweep of human history. The Security Council has just referred crimes in Darfur to the new International Criminal Court. In 1990, no leader would have had any cause to worry about international accountability for criminally brutalizing his own people. Today, no leader anywhere in the world can bank on impunity based on sovereignty. This is a profound change in an astonishingly short period of time.

42

The anomalies killing nonproliferation

The International Herald Tribune, 18 May 2005

The Nuclear Non-Proliferation Treaty (NPT) is the most successful arms control agreement in history. Yet eminent commentators warn that it is in grave danger of erosion and complete collapse leading to a cascade of proliferation.

The diplomats gathered for a month in New York to review the treaty face difficulties rooted in six major anomalies.

First, the definition of a nuclear weapons state is chronological – a country that manufactured and exploded a nuclear device before 1 January 1967. India, Pakistan and Israel could test, deploy and even use nuclear weapons, but cannot be described as nuclear powers. In principle, Britain and France could dismantle their nuclear edifice and destroy their nuclear arsenals, but would still count as nuclear powers.

This is an Alice in Wonderland approach to affairs of deadly seriousness. But can the treaty definition be opened up for revision through a formal amendment of the 188-member document with all the unpredictable consequences? If not, whither realism?

Second, even as the threat from nonstate actors has grown frighteningly real, multilateral treaties like this one can regulate and monitor the activities only of states. Abdul Qadeer Khan's underground nuclear bazaar showed how porous the border is between private and state rogue actors. A robust and credible normative architecture to control the actions of terrorist groups that can acquire nuclear weapons must be developed outside the nonproliferation treaty.

Third, the cases of Israel, India, Iran, Libya, Pakistan and North Korea show that decades after a problem arises, we still cannot agree on an appropriate response inside the NPT framework.

Significant gaps exist in the legal and institutional framework to combat today's real threats. It is impossible to defang tyrants of their nuclear weapons the day after they acquire and use them. The United Nations seems incapable of doing so the day before: the Security Council can hardly table the North Korean threat for discussion and resolution.

The fourth anomaly is lumping biological, chemical and nuclear weapons in one conceptual and policy basket. They differ in their technical features, in the ease with they can be acquired and developed, and in their capacity to cause mass destruction. Treating them as one weapons category can distort analysis and produce flawed responses.

There is the related danger of mission creep. The taboo against the use of nuclear weapons is so strong that it is hard to imagine their employment other than against enemy nuclear weapons. The creeping tendency to redefine their mission to counter all weapons of mass destruction weakens the nuclear taboo and allows the nuclear powers to obfuscate the reality that they are the possessors of the most potent of those weapons. If nuclear weapons are accepted as having a role to counter biochemical warfare, then how can we deny a nuclear-weapons capability to Iran, which has actually suffered chemical weapons attacks?

Fifth, the five nuclear powers preach but do not practice nuclear abstinence. It defies history, common sense and logic to believe that a self-selecting group of five countries can keep a permanent monopoly on the world's most destructive weaponry. Not a single country that had nuclear weapons when the NPT was signed in 1968 has given them up. Their behaviour fuels the politics of grievance and resentment.

Can the country with the world's most powerful nuclear weapons rightfully use military force to prevent their acquisition by others? The logics of nuclear disarmament and nonproliferation are inseparable. Hence the axiom of nonproliferation: As long as any one country has them, others, including terrorist groups, will try their best (or worst) to get them.

The final paradox concerns the contradiction between rhetoric and example. It is not possible to convince others of the futility of nuclear weapons when the facts of continued possession and doctrines and threats of use prove their utility for some. Refining and miniaturizing nuclear weapons, developing new doctrines and justifications for their use, and lowering the threshold of their employment weaken the taboo against them and erode the normative barriers to nuclear proliferation.

Are these anomalies so few in number and so lightweight that they can be accommodated within auxiliary arrangements inside the nonproliferation treaty?

Or are they such big problems that the treaty will grind to a halt and be replaced? The negotiators in New York have their work cut out for them.

43

Absolute security neither possible nor desirable

The Canberra Times, 29 July 2005

Last Saturday, Jean Charles de Menezes, a young Brazilian legally living and working in Britain, was killed at a London Tube station in a tragic case of mistaken identity. Police have confirmed he had no links whatsoever to terrorism. But he had come out of a house under surveillance by anti-terrorist undercover police, was overdressed on a warm day, ran in panic when challenged by the police, and was shot seven times at point-blank range.[1] Perhaps he had suspicious wires sticking out: turns out he was an electrician. From his perspective, in the heightened state of fear in London, perhaps he ran because a group of suspicious young stalkers were chasing him.

Sympathy for the police dilemma is tempered by still greater sympathy for Menezes. The case highlights the need for a proper balance between civil liberties, human rights and the responsibility of the state to protect its citizens from terrorists.

Before 9/11, Westerners were prone to ambivalence between terrorists and governments fighting to maintain national security and assure public safety. After 9/11, they began to view other countries' parallel wars against terrorism through the prism of a fellow-government facing agonizing policy choices in the real world, rather than single-issue groups whose vision is not anchored in any responsibility for policy decisions.

But no government has a licence to kill. The death of Menezes is a victory for the terrorists. Success in defeating terrorism requires us to be true to our values that they reject. Michael Ignatieff has argued for the lesser evil of curtailing liberties and using violence in order to defeat the greater evil of terrorism. But we must be careful not to succumb to the still greater evil of destroying the very values for which democracies stand. The way to do this is to require of governments that they justify all restrictive measures publicly, submit them to judicial review and circumscribe them with sunset clauses to guard against the temporary becoming permanent.

Many democracies have shifted the balance of laws and administrative practices towards state security. A CIA counter-terrorism expert testified that "After 9/11 the gloves came off," while another US official remarked that "if you don't violate someone's human rights, you aren't doing your job." There developed also the distasteful practice of "rendition to torture," sending prisoners to other countries precisely because the latter were known to practice torture as a routine repertoire of interrogation. In Australia, the post-9/11 hysteria was harvested by the government to introduce tough detention laws against illegal immigrants in defence of a policy of Fortress Australia that led to the detention of 33 Australian citizens, one of whom was deported to her country of birth and another, a mentally ill woman, spent 10 months in detention.

Terrorism has a threefold impact on human rights. It is itself an extreme denial of the most basic human right to life, and it creates an environment in which people cannot live in freedom from fear and enjoy other rights. Second, the threat of terrorism can be used by governments to enact laws that strip away many civil liberties and political freedoms. One common technique is to reverse the burden of proof: those accused of terrorist activities, sympathies or even guilt by association on the basis of accusations by anonymous people are to be presumed to be guilty until they can prove their innocence of unspecified charges. Third, without necessarily amending laws or enacting new ones, governments can use the need to fight terrorism as an alibi to stifle dissent and criticism and imprison or threaten domestic opponents.

President Bush's response to 9/11 was to elevate terrorism from a tactic or a method into a transcendental conflict: an epic struggle of historic proportions between the greatest force for good on earth, responding to a calling from beyond the stars, against enemies bent on destroying it. Neutrality was not an option. But this Manichean reinterpretation of 9/11 emboldened many other governments to re-label their domestic difficulties as part of the global war on terror.

The robustness and resilience of the democracies' commitment to human rights norms and values will be judged in the final analysis not by the breaches in the aftermath of 9/11, Bali and London, but by the reversal and attenuation of the breaches through judicial and political processes as well as the pressure of domestic and international civil society.

We must not privilege security and order to such an extent as to destroy our most cherished values of liberty and justice in the search for an unattainable absolute security.

Islam is a religion of peace. Muslims should reclaim their religion from the fanatics. No excuses, no alibis, no mantras of one man's terrorist is another man's freedom fighter. Tough on terrorists, yes. But tough also on the causes of terrorism and in defence of the virtues of tolerance, human rights and civil liberties.

Note

1. Some of the information as given out by the police initially was subsequently shown to have been wrong in crucial respects.

44

NPT regime in crisis after failed NY confab

The Daily Yomiuri, 1 August 2005

The Nuclear Non-Proliferation Treaty (NPT) is the centrepiece of the global nonproliferation regime that codified the international political norm of non-nuclear-weapons status. Sixty years after the Hiroshima and Nagasaki atomic bombings, the NPT regime faces a fourfold crisis.

Some countries are engaged in undeclared nuclear activities in violation of their nonproliferation obligations. Others have failed to honour their disarmament obligations. A third group – India, Israel and Pakistan – are nuclear-weapon states outside the NPT. Finally, nonstate actors like terrorist groups are seeking to acquire nuclear weapons.

Arms control agreements are multilaterally negotiated outcomes among governments entailing difficult technical and political judgments on reciprocity, mutuality and relative balance. They are achievable if countries engage in a genuine give-and-take where the final outcome satisfies the minimum requirements of all without necessarily achieving the maximum goal of any. But they prove a mirage when the basic minimum interests of key parties are too far apart to be bridged.

The United Nations seems to be moribund as a forum for negotiating arms control and disarmament treaties. The seventh NPT Review Conference, held at the United Nations in New York, ended in complete collapse in May. It failed to address the vital challenges or offer practical ideas for preventing the use, acquisition and spread of nuclear weapons.

The first half of the conference was dogged by procedural wrangling and the second was rancorous. The exercise ended in acrimony and recriminations over where the primary blame lay for the lost opportunity to bolster the NPT.

Washington, which has historically led international efforts to reinforce the NPT, faulted the international community, yet again, for failure to confront the reality of the threat of proliferation by countries like Iran and North Korea. It will likely retreat even more strongly into extra-UN multilateral efforts like the Proliferation Security Initiative, in which more than 60 countries are cooperating on monitoring and, if necessary, interdicting the illicit trade in nuclear materials.

Arms control advocates countered that the US delegation had come intent on focusing on the proliferation side of the equation and was totally intransigent with regard to existing disarmament measures.

Most countries concluded that the nuclear powers had no intention of fulfilling their NPT-based disarmament obligations and agreed commitments from the 1995 and 2000 conferences. This had a triple negative effect: it eroded support for US proposals for strengthening the nonproliferation elements of the treaty, weakened support for strong action against possible Iranian and North Korean transgressions, and may soften adherence to NPT obligations over the long run.

The NPT was signed in 1968 and came into force in 1970. Unusually among such international agreements, it required a conference to be held after 25 years to discuss whether to renew the treaty indefinitely or for further fixed periods. The 1995 conference decided to renew the NPT indefinitely, and in doing so enshrined a strong international legal bulwark against nuclear nonproliferation. The president of that conference was the Sri Lankan diplomat Jayantha Dhanapala.

Newton Bowles, a distinguished Canadian diplomat who was involved with the United Nations in many capacities from its start, notes in his memoir *The Diplomacy of Hope* that Dhanapala "left a legacy of intellectual rigor and moral commitment" as under-secretary-general for disarmament (1998–2003). Dhanapala has now written his own account of the 1995 event, *Multilateral Diplomacy and the NPT: An Insider's Account*.

While the 1975 and 1985 review conferences produced final documents, the 1980 and 1990 conferences failed to do so. Of the 178 parties to the NPT at the time, 175 attended the 1995 review and extension conference. The timing was good: there was still a residue of optimism from the ending of the Cold War and goodwill towards Moscow and Washington, who were finally cutting back their nuclear stockpiles.

By contrast this year's review came after two successful conferences, and so the cycle of alternating success and failure pointed to problems. More importantly, the US mood was completely different, both because of 9/11 and a growing hubris of exceptionalism. The terrorist attacks of 11 September 2001 hardened the edge of US foreign policy and freed Washington from a sense of having to make any concessions to multilateralism.

Dhanapala wrote that 1995 proved "that large multilateral conferences could be concluded on time, with a positive result, and without acrimony and divisive voting." If so, 2005 proves that such conferences cannot be self-guaranteeing. Skilful and decisive conference management is surely a prerequisite, since any large gathering can founder under an incompetent chairman.

In addition, there has to be an objective base of overlapping and compatible interests. Simply providing tables and chairs in congenial surroundings cannot compensate for deep divisions over the substance of the work agenda. This was the real problem in 2005: the worldviews of some of the nuclear powers proved fundamentally antagonistic to those of others.

The NPT provided for a vote on extension if necessary. In the end in 1995 the decision was made by consensus, and Dhanapala credits this for the spirit of harmony that prevailed. But one could also conclude that the possibility of a vote if necessary concentrates the mind of holdouts.

Absent that, the procedural requirement for consensus means that spoilers can wreck any collective decision-making forum, confident that they will not face the humiliation of a vote proving just how isolated their position is. This has an echo today in UN Secretary-General Kofi Annan's call for an early decision on some UN Security Council reform, preferably by consensus, but by vote if necessary. The Group of Four, including Japan, support this.

Dhanapala was prescient in warning, in his closing speech on 12 May 1995, that the indefinite extension of the treaty should not be construed as "a permanence of unbalanced obligations." The conference's "unmistakable message" was that "nonproliferation and disarmament can be pursued only jointly, not at each other's expense."

The trouble is, due to a changed worldview, Washington has moved away from that package, and who's to say it is wrong? It believes that the threats have changed in nature and gravity, the world is a harsher place than originally believed at the end of the Cold War, and international pressures to fulfil earlier commitments can be more easily deflected and should be more firmly rebuffed.

Yet, ironically, the failure of the 2005 conference means that the agreed commitments from 1995 and 2000 remain in force. The revenge perhaps of history that refuses to end?

45

UN's "Einstein" moment

The Japan Times, 3 October 2005

The optimists had hoped for a "San Francisco moment" in New York, as decisive and momentous as the signing of the UN Charter 60 years earlier in the city by the bay. Critics might well conclude that instead the United Nations had an Einstein moment, recalling his definition of madness as doing something over and over again and expecting a different result each time. The organization has been a graveyard of every previous major reform effort.

Shaken by Iraq and beset by allegations of fraud and mismanagement, UN Secretary-General Kofi Annan brought together a group of 16 distinguished experts to probe the nature and gravity of today's threats and recommend collective solutions to them through a reformed United Nations. Saying that he had "resisted the temptation to include all areas in which progress is important or desirable" in order to concentrate on items on which "action is both vital and achievable," Annan drew on its report to present "an agenda of highest priorities" for forging a new consensus on key challenges and collective action.

With respect to internal conflicts, the high-level panel argued, and Annan agreed, that "the issue is not the 'right to intervene' of any state, but the 'responsibility to protect' of every state." This is one of the few substantive items to survive. The summit's "outcome document" contains acceptance of the new norm of the responsibility to protect populations from genocide, war crimes, ethnic cleansing and crimes against humanity, and willingness to take timely and decisive action through the Security Council when peaceful means prove inadequate and national authorities are manifestly failing to do it. I have a proprietary interest in this norm as a member of the international commission that promulgated it, and as one of the principal authors of the report.

Both the panel and Annan proposed a simple definition of terrorism. Its focus on the nature of the acts breaks the unhelpful link with causes and motivations. The proposed definition brought clarity and rigor, removed the ideological edge from the debate and muted the charges of inconsistency and double standards.

Because terrorism deliberately targets civilians to achieve political goals, it always represents a conscious choice of one tactic over others. The strong condemnation of terrorism "in all its forms and manifestations," no matter what the cause, is reiterated in the outcome document. The call for a comprehensive convention is endorsed. But there is no agreed definition.

The triple crisis of nuclear weapons arises from noncompliance with obligations of the Nuclear Non-Proliferation Treaty (NPT) by some states engaged in undeclared nuclear activities and others that have failed to honour their disarmament obligations; states that are not party to the NPT; and nonstate actors seeking to acquire nuclear weapons. Annan warned that "Progress in both disarmament and nonproliferation is essential and neither should be held hostage to the other."

The NPT Review Conference in May collapsed into complete failure. The summit failed to come to any agreement on nonproliferation and disarmament, a failure described as "inexcusable" and "a disgrace" by Annan. More and more countries are bumping against the nuclear-weapons ceiling at the same time as the world energy crisis is encouraging a move to nuclear energy.

There is agreement on a weakened Human Rights Council and Peace-building Commission, and on "early reform" of the Security Council through continued efforts. After a decade of talks, they agreed to talk some more. And they wonder why the United Nations is falling into disrepute.

There are two possible explanations for the underwhelming outcome, one cynical, the other charitable. For a UN official, it is a toss-up as to which is the more dispiriting.

The cynical explanation is that all sides pushed their own interests, blocked items not of interest to them, and criticized others for not elevating the common interest. While pushing items of importance to themselves, they rejected others as not being all that urgent and distracting attention from their own pet reforms.

Canada's Paul Martin expressed "profound disappointment" at the failure to agree on an operational and powerful human rights council and criticized the fondness for "empty rhetoric" over concrete results, ignoring Canadians' spoiler role in thwarting an enlarged permanent membership of the Security Council.

South Africa's Thabo Mbeki criticized "rich and powerful nations" for blocking attempts to widen the Security Council to include more developing nations, ignoring how the head of momentum built by the G-4 (Brazil, Germany, India and Japan) was stalled by the African Union's insistence on full veto powers for all new permanent members. Washington wanted to focus on nonproliferation and management reform, but betrayed an instinct for mismanaging international diplomacy in presenting a list of demands for hundreds of amendments at the 11th hour to a text that had been under negotiation for months, and in the refusal to link nonproliferation to disarmament.

But Americans have yet to receive a convincing answer as to why the world's only superpower should acquiesce in its own "Gulliverization," bound and tethered by the many fine strands of international treaties and conventions. Or why they should not seek to refashion institutions to reflect their preeminence. Or why indeed the growing circle of democratic countries should accept moral equivalence with regimes which are anything but when it comes to collective decision-making.

Westerners blamed the developing countries for blocking efforts at management reform that would give greater discretionary authority to the secretary-general in hiring and firing UN personnel. This ignores how the senior ranks of the UN system are already disproportionately dominated by Westerners. Developing countries fear that Americans and Europeans would commandeer even more positions if the General Assembly surrendered its prerogatives.

The charitable interpretation is that the sense of shared values and solidarity that makes up an international community may have frayed a thread too far. UN membership has not just quadrupled since 1945, but grown far more diverse. There are many more states today, with markedly diverging interests and perspectives. The range of issues they have to confront are more numerous, complex and challenging, for example, hot button items like global warming, HIV/AIDS and nuclear terrorism that were not on the international agenda in 1945. There are also many more non-state actors.

A "community" exists if members share core values and agree on legitimate behaviour. The struggle for UN reform is a battle over policy, not just process and management. Should it be the forum of choice or last resort for collective-action solutions to global problems: less or more environmental regulation, nonproliferation and/or disarmament, counterterrorism vs. human rights, a strong state that provides social protection and regulation or an unobtrusive state that lets capital and markets rule? It is a struggle between international Keynesianism and neoliberalism.

The serious disagreements between the countries of the world on the answers to these questions and other key issues may be evidence of the growing loss, not betrayal, of the sense of international community on which the United Nations is predicated.

46

National security? It's time to think about human security

The Globe and Mail, 17 October 2005

In June 2004, Walter Maestri, the emergency management chief in New Orleans's Jefferson Parish, pleaded for federal assistance in completing the area's levees. As he explained to the *Times-Picayune* newspaper, the president's budget appeared to have moved funding for the levees to funding for national security efforts such as the war in Iraq. He said that, for the people of New Orleans, the levees are part and parcel of their security because they help protect them 365 days a year. Hurricane Katrina thus joins last year's devastating Asian tsunami as reasons for re-framing "security" in human terms.

The concept of human security puts the individual at the centre of the debate. Its fundamental component – the security of people against threats to personal safety and life – can be put at risk by external aggression, but also by factors within a country. The reformulation of national security into human security is simple, yet has profound consequences for how we see the world, how we organize our political affairs, how we make choices in public and foreign policy, and how we relate to fellow human beings from many different countries and civilizations.

Its significance is underlined in a major new report being launched at the United Nations today. It's the most comprehensive review of global security trends yet published. The Human Security Report, compiled by Andrew Mack, a former UN official now at the University of British Columbia, contains some startlingly good news that should help offset the prevailing pessimism on the state of the world and the United Nations' performance in protecting peace and promoting progress.

Conflicts, it seems, are down 40 percent since 1992; the deadliest conflicts (those with more than 1,000 battle-deaths) are down by 80 percent. Nearly 700,000 people in total were killed in battle in 1950; in 2002, the figure was 20,000. The average number of those killed per battle in 1950 was 38,000; in 2002, it was only 600 per battle.

Unlike previous wars between big mechanized armies, today's typical wars are fought in poor countries with small arms and light weapons between weak government forces and ill-trained rebels. In most cases, such as in Darfur, disease and malnutrition resulting from warfare kill far more people than missiles, bombs and bullets.

Wars have also shifted locale since 1945, from East Asia until the mid-1970s, to the Middle East, Central and South Asia in the 1980s and sub-Saharan Africa today.

Africa's armed conflicts are particularly difficult to avoid, contain or end because of pervasive poverty, declining GDP per capita, reduced aid, poor infrastructure, weak administration, external intervention, an abundance of cheap weapons and a bitter legacy of past wars. Moreover, violent conflicts in Africa exacerbate the very conditions that gave rise to them in the first place, creating a classic "conflict trap" from which escape is difficult.

Genocides, international crises and military coups are dramatically down, too. And human-rights abuses have declined in five out of six regions in the developing world since the mid-1990s. International terrorist attacks are becoming more numerous and deadly, yet fewer than 1,000 people a year on average have been killed by international terrorists over the past 30 years, a fraction of those killed in warfare.

Despite these positive changes, the report warns against complacency. There are still 60 armed conflicts raging around the globe, gross abuses of human rights, widespread war crimes and ever-deadlier acts of terrorism. The underlying causes of conflict are rarely addressed, so the risk of new wars breaking out and old ones restarting remains real. Almost half of all peace agreements collapse into conflict within five years. That the world is becoming more peaceful is no consolation to those suffering in Darfur, Iraq, Nepal, Indonesia or New Orleans.

The reality of human insecurity cannot be wished away. To many poor people in the world's poorest countries, the risk of being attacked by terrorists or with weapons of mass destruction is far removed from the pervasive reality of the "soft threats" – hunger, lack of safe drinking water and sanitation and endemic diseases. These threats are neither unconnected to peace and security, nor can they be ignored until the hard threats have been taken care of.

Three years in the making, the Human Security Report will be widely welcomed as the most authoritative compilation of data and analysis of key trends. As proven by the shifting of funds from building levees in New Orleans to bridges in Alaska, and the redeployment of National Guards to Iraq, policy choices can have deadly consequences. This is why human security is as much a policy as a conceptual template.

47

The reduction of impunity

The Japan Times, 10 November 2005

Government is about making and implementing public policy choices. These are neither always easy nor always right. Governments, like individuals, do make mistakes. But in democracies, the task of making decisions on behalf of the people is delegated to elected representatives who then answer to the courts on constitutionality and to the people on the consequences of their choices.

At the same time, every society, including international society, always has some members whose intellectual conceit and moral arrogance lead them to want to substitute their judgment for the outcome of the democratic process.

David Forsythe of the University of Nebraska uses the phrase "judicial romanticism" for the idea of always looking to courts for a solution to every problem. In the commitment to justice at any price, the romanticists discount political and diplomatic alternatives. In the United States, President Richard Nixon would have been prosecuted for Watergate.

I saw this romanticism in action in New Zealand in the mid-1980s when many were unhappy that the government succumbed to French economic pressure and released the intelligence agents convicted of the *Rainbow Warrior* bombing.

Not everyone in South Africa was happy with the amnesty granted to some apartheid-era criminals by the Truth and Reconciliation Commission. Some in Britain would like to see Irish Republican Army terrorists brought to book even at the cost of imperilling the peace accords.

And we see it within East Timor in calls for no compromise with the murderers of 1999.

Romanticism turns into judicial colonialism with demands that the political and diplomatic decisions made by democratically elected governments of other countries be subordinated to "international" judicial processes that reflect the values of the most dominant countries of the day.

It is based in moral imperialism: our values are so manifestly superior to theirs that we have the right to impose it on them.

To appreciate this, consider two examples in the contrary direction. It is possible for reasonable people to disagree on the rights and wrongs of homosexuality and abortion. Both acts are prohibited in many countries, perhaps accounting for a majority of the world's population. Would those countries be justified in insisting that their moral position on homosexuality must be written into the domestic laws of Western countries? If so, is this an example of moral imperialism?

And, if they had the economic and military muscle, would strongly pro-life countries have the right – nay, the moral duty, in the language of the humanitarian warriors – to coerce us into ending the killing of thousands of innocent lives every year by taking doctors and women to criminal courts? If so, is this an example of judicial colonialism?

Unlike domestic society, we lack functioning mechanisms of judicial accountability in world affairs. Some day hopefully every tyrant and warmonger will be hauled before international criminal courts. The UN Charter was never meant to be a tyrant's charter of impunity or his constitutional instrument of choice for self-protection.

The Holocaust in which several million Jews were systematically killed in the Nazi program to exterminate them – the familiar cycle of pogroms modernized into industrialized and highly efficient mass slaughter – retains a unique emotional resonance. But repeating the slogan of "Never Again" requires chutzpah after the repeats of the horror of mass killings in Rwanda, Srebrenica, Darfur and elsewhere.

Much as humanitarians might want to believe that they still hold up the virtue of truth to the vice of power, the truth is that the vocabulary of virtue has just as often been appropriated in the service of power. Nuremberg and Tokyo were instances of victors' justice. Yet by historical standards, both tribunals were remarkable for giving defeated leaders the opportunity to defend their actions in a court of law instead of being dispatched for summary execution.

The ad hoc tribunals of the 1990s for Rwanda and the former Yugoslavia are important milestones in efforts to fill institutional gaps in international criminal justice. They have been neither unqualified successes nor total failures. While the international criminal tribunals have primacy over the operation of domestic court systems, the International Criminal Court has been constructed to give primacy to domestic systems and become operative only in the event of domestic unwillingness or incapacity.

After the Iraq war started in 2003, British Prime Minister Tony Blair and his defence and foreign ministers were accused of crimes against humanity by Greek lawyers who lodged a case with the International Criminal Court (ICC) on 28 July 2003. The doctrine of universal jurisdiction was employed also to threaten prosecution against US President George W. Bush and Gen. Tommy Franks (commander of the US forces in Iraq).

Defense Secretary Donald Rumsfeld retaliated by warning that if US officials could no longer travel to Brussels without fear of prosecution, North Atlantic Treaty Organization headquarters would clearly have to be relocated to another country. In July 2003 Belgium amended its controversial law on universal jurisdiction and restricted trials in Belgian courts to crimes committed or suffered by its citizens or residents.

Truth commissions provide a halfway house between victors' or foreigners' justice and collective amnesia. The ad hoc tribunals have helped to bring hope and justice to some victims, combat the impunity of some perpetrators and greatly enrich the jurisprudence of international criminal and humanitarian law. But they have been expensive, time-consuming and contributed little to sustainable national capacities for justice administration. Truth commissions take a victim-centred approach, help to establish a historical record and contribute to memorializing defining epochs in a nation's history.

The ethic of conviction would impose obligations to prosecute people for their past criminal misdeeds to the full extent of the law. The ethic of responsibility imposes the countervailing requirement to judge the wisdom of alternative courses of action with respect to their consequences for social harmony in the future.

Of the four sets of actors in global governance, nongovernmental organizations remain more fiercely resistant to calls for independent accountability for the consequences of their actions than governments, international organizations and multinational corporations. The fault line between activists and policymakers is no longer as sharp as it used to be.

Harvard University's David Kennedy argues that humanitarian actors often deny the reality of bad consequences flowing from good intentions. Humanitarian actors are participants in global governance as advocates, activists and policymakers. Their critiques and policy prescriptions have demonstrable consequences. With influence over policy should come responsibility for the consequences of policy.

The ICC offers hope for a permanent reduction in the phenomenon of impunity. In 1990, a tyrant would have been reasonably confident of escaping international accountability for any atrocities. Today, there is no guarantee of prosecution and accountability, but not a single brutish ruler can be confident of escaping international justice. The certainty of impunity is gone. Fifteen years is a very short time in the broad sweep of history for such a dramatic transformation of the international criminal landscape.

48

US-India nuclear accord a win-win outcome for all

The Daily Yomiuri, 27 November 2005

The bilateral agreement between India and the United States on civilian nuclear cooperation, signed during Indian Prime Minister Manmohan Singh's visit to Washington on 18 July, remains contentious. Yet it serves the strategic goals of both countries while also advancing the global non-proliferation agenda more realistically than any conceivable alternative.

To single issue activists – those dismissed as "nonproliferation ayatol-lahs" by Indian diplomats – the agreement is a sellout that will only make it more difficult to secure Nuclear Non-Proliferation Treaty (NPT) compliance from other proliferators. They are lobbying the US Congress to block the deal, or at least to seek much more substantial concessions from New Delhi. India voted once with Washington in the International Atomic Energy Agency on Iranian noncompliance with the NPT. But where is the guarantee that it will do so again? In the meantime, Tehran is already pointing to the sweetheart deal with New Delhi as yet another example of double standards whereby Washington discriminates against Muslim countries.

To Indian hawks with a single minded focus on rapidly expanding and modernizing India's nuclear weapons capability, the agreement is a sell-out that will significantly constrain India's nuclear options in asymmetric comparison to the freedoms of the five NPT-licit nuclear powers. They want to embarrass the Indian government into repudiating the deal. India has secured only promises of future assistance that is subject to all the unpredictable vagaries of Congress.[1]

In the meantime, its vote on Iran overturned three long-standing major

planks of Indian foreign policy: the NPT is illegitimate because discriminatory; no country can be bound to obligations arising from international
agreements that it has not signed (the International Atomic Energy
Agency model additional protocol); and the unreformed UN Security
Council is itself illegitimate because it is an unreconstructed vestige of
1945.

The passion, depth of anger and strength of opposition to the vote
among allies within the ruling coalition government as well as in the opposition parties must have shaken the government.

Washington has three strategic goals riding on the agreement. The
first, with a long historical pedigree, is preventing the emergence of
China as a regional hegemon. The second is courting India as a populous,
democratic and friendly rising power. (Unlike the postmodern militaries
of many European allies, the million-man Indian Army actually fights,
says Robert Blackwill, former US ambassador to India.) And the third is
drawing India, which is not party to global nuclear arms control agreements, into the web of nonproliferation obligations through verifiable bilateral commitments instead of unilateral policy. Blackwill notes that the
administration of US President George W. Bush sees India as "a strategic opportunity and not a constantly irritating recalcitrant" whereas for
the Clinton administration it was "a persistent nonproliferation problem
that required an American-imposed solution."

The result? New Delhi-Washington relations are the best they've ever
been.

India's strategic goals dovetail with these, including deepening New
Delhi-Washington ties without courting client-status dependency. New
Delhi also has an additional strategic goal, to ensure energy security by
investing heavily in nuclear power.

The last few years have shown just how easy it is for determined countries, even relatively minor ones, to evade international restrictions on
the proliferation of sensitive material, infrastructure development and
other activities. Given India's size, resilience, know-how and sophisticated technical capacity, driving it into the ranks of the rogue proliferators would be foolish. No one has produced a realistic roadmap of why
and how India would give up its nuclear option unless it is part of a
global deal to eliminate nuclear weapons totally, which is not going to
happen anytime soon.

Of the proliferation-sensitive countries, India and Israel are exceptional in their proven track records as responsible stewards of indigenous
nuclear capabilities. Both are long-term democracies with civilians in
charge of government policy. Both live in highly unstable and volatile
geostrategic environments. And both have been victims of numerous
terrorist attacks over the past decade. To equate them morally with all

other problem countries, on the simplistic argument that nonproliferation trumps every single other consideration, is unhelpful to advancing any policy goal, including nonproliferation (for the reasons given above).

If indeed nuclear weapons themselves are the problem, rather than their possession by irresponsible powers, then the policy goal should be their total and verifiable elimination from the arsenals of all countries. Alternatively, if some countries are more responsible than others as safe-guarded possessors of nuclear knowledge, material and weapons, then this requires a discriminatory calculation that is unlikely to see India and Israel lumped with the potential rogue regimes. Unlike them, India and Israel have not violated NPT obligations, for they have none.

The nuclear ambitions of North Korea and Iran (and of Iraq in the past) go back several decades and have never had India as their principal benchmark. India's pursuit of the nuclear option outside the NPT frame-work also stretches back over many decades. Other countries have signed the NPT because they believe it to be in their national interest. India has remained outside the NPT because it believed otherwise. The bilateral agreement with Washington is its first tangible integration into the global nonproliferation regime. This is an advance on the existing unsatisfactory status quo, not a setback.

Note

1. The exemption to domestic US law to enable the deal to proceed was passed by Congress and signed by President George W. Bush in December 2006.

49

Why America needs the UN

The Japan Times, 26 January 2006

We have to live in and manage a world in which the threat and use of force remain an ever present reality. The material capacity, economic efficiency, political organization and military skills in the use of force determine the international power hierarchy. Great powers rise and fall on the tide of history. Rivalry between them caused two world wars in the last century that strengthened the determination to tame the use of military force as an accepted part of sovereign statehood. The right to wage war in self-defence was kept by states, but otherwise the decision to authorize wars was restricted to the United Nations.

The conviction was that for peace to be maintained, the United Nations must be able and willing to use force in the name of the international community against outlaw states. This proved unduly optimistic. Instead the typical UN deployment of military troops took the form of "peace operations," not military combat missions.

The California-based Rand Corporation undertook a comparative study of US combat and UN peace operations: *America's Role in Nation-Building: From Germany to Iraq* (2003) and *The UN's Role in Nation-Building: From the Congo to Iraq* (2005). Its conclusions reinforce the need for complementary operations based on comparative advantage.

The United Nations is better at low-profile, small-footprint operations where soft-power assets of international legitimacy and local impartiality compensate for hard-power deficit. The quality of UN peacekeeping troops, police officers and civilian administrators is more uneven and has become worse with the retrenchment of Western nations from UN operations, and their arrival on the scene is often tardy.

Military reversals are less damaging to the United Nations because military force is not the source of its credibility, whereas they strike at the core basis of US influence. To overcome domestic scepticism, American policymakers define overseas missions in grandiloquent terms and make the operations hostage to their own rhetoric, while UN missions are outcomes of highly negotiated, densely bureaucratic and much more circumspect documents.

Because member states are unwilling to contribute more manpower or money, UN operations tend to be undermanned and under-resourced, deploying small and weak forces into, hopefully, post-conflict situations under best-case assumptions. If the assumptions prove false, the forces are reinforced, withdrawn or rescued. Washington deploys troops under worst-case assumptions with overwhelming force to establish a secure environment quickly.

The United States spent $4.5 billion per month in Iraq in 2004, compared to under $4 billion per year for all 17 UN missions combined. This does not mean that the United Nations could do the job in Iraq better, more efficiently or more cheaply. It does mean that there were at least 17 other places where Washington did not face calls to intervene because the United Nations was already doing the job. The total number of UN peacekeepers – around 65,000 – is modest by the standards of US expeditionary capability. But it is more than any other country or coalition can field.

UN missions have been relatively more successful – a higher proportion of local countries have been left in peaceful and democratic conditions than with US operations. This could be a statistical artifice: a different selection of cases might produce different results. Or it could indicate that the US operations have been intrinsically more difficult, requiring larger forces, more robust mandates and greater combat weight.

Or it could even be that the United Nations has been better at learning lessons. James Dobbins, the lead author of the Rand study, notes that Kofi Annan, when he moved to New York as secretary-general, retained many of his staff from his days as head of UN peacekeeping in key advisory positions. This offset many institutional discontinuities. By contrast, says Dobbins, Washington tends to staff each new operation as if it were its first and is destined to be its last.

The UN and US roles complement each other in managing the messy conflicts around the world. Peace operations enlarge the spectrum of capabilities available to the international community to respond to threats of chaos in the periphery. But the United Nations does not have its own military and police forces and would be hard pressed to achieve anything notable without active US engagement, let alone against its vital interests and determined opposition. UN operations allow Washington to choose how, where and how deeply to engage in different conflicts around the world.

Participation in UN peace operations symbolizes solidarity and shared responsibility. If the United Nations is unable or unwilling to honour its responsibility to protect victims of genocide, ethnic cleansing or other egregious humanitarian atrocities, Washington can forge multilateral co-alitions of the willing to lead military interventions to stop the atrocities.

The Brahimi Report (2000) reinforced the importance of a UN-authorized force under the active leadership of a significant military power. For while the Security Council can validate the legitimacy of a peace-support operation, the United Nations does not have enough pro-fessionally trained and equipped troops and police forces of its own. Suc-cessful operations that need robust mandates might still have to depend on coalitions of the able and willing – but also duly authorized.

For decades, UN peace operations have served US security interests in the Middle East, Africa, Central America, Southeast Asia and Haiti. Peacekeeping will remain the United Nations' instrument of choice for engaging with the typical conflicts in today's world. The US approach to peace operations will therefore continue to define the nature of the US engagement with the United Nations. Because the United States will re-main the main financial underwriter of the costs of UN peacekeeping, it will continue to exercise unmatched influence on the establishment, man-date, nature, size, and termination of UN peace operations.

By their very nature, they cannot produce conclusive results either on the battlefield – they are peace operations, not war – or around the nego-tiating table – they are military deployments, not diplomatic talks. A drawdown of UN peace operations would reduce US leverage in spread-ing the burden of providing international security and lessening the de-mands and expectations on the United States to take up the slack.

Conversely, scapegoating the United Nations will erode its legitimacy and so reduce the US ability to use the United Nations in pursuit of other US goals – for example in enforcing nonproliferation.

To die-hard UN-bashers and passers, Washington needs the United Nations like fish need bicycles. The facts say otherwise.

50

UN, US should not work at cross-purposes

The Daily Yomiuri, 1 May 2006

The United Nations and the United States come together at the cross-roads of ideals and power politics. The world is a better and safer place for all of us (1) because the Cold War was fought, how it was fought, and who won – US power prevailing in defence of US values; and (2) because the United Nations exists, what it does, and what it symbolizes – the ideal of an international society rooted in human solidarity, based in law and ruled by reason. Therefore the world will be a better and safer place for all of us if the indispensable superpower and the indispensable international organization work in tandem, not at cross-purposes.

Ideas are the currency of an information society and knowledge economy, and institutions are conduits for ideas. In the broad sweep of history, empires rise and fall, rulers come and go. They are remembered chiefly for the ideas they leave behind, embedded in institutions or practices, for improved governance or quality of life. Over the course of the last two centuries, the idea of an international community bound together by shared values, benefits and responsibilities, and common rules and procedures, took hold of peoples' imagination.

The United Nations is the institutional embodiment of that development. In this sense it is the repository of international idealism, the belief that human beings belong to one family, inhabit the same planet and have joint custodial responsibility to preserve the peace, promote human rights, husband resources and protect the environment. The global public good of peace and prosperity cannot be achieved by any country acting on its own. Under conditions of modern civilization, no country is an island sufficient unto itself anymore.

9/11 was a decisive repudiation of the belief that the most powerful country ever in human history can shelter behind supposedly impregnable lines of continental defence. Yet while the terrorists destroyed the World Trade Center, caused some damage to the Pentagon, and shook US self-confidence momentarily, they did not and cannot destroy the idea and symbolism of the United States: The metaphor of the shining city on the hill burning bright with the hopes of all mankind, in particular the oppressed, the downtrodden and the outcasts – in the immortal words of Abraham Lincoln, a nation "conceived in liberty, and dedicated to the proposition that all men are created equal." It has been the particular genius of the United States to welcome the despised and discarded dregs of other societies, to offer them the chance to live the American dream, to watch their dreams turn into reality, and then to harness those dreams to forge the most prosperous and the most powerful nation on Earth.

Therein lies the rub. Because of the sustaining belief in being a virtuous power, the United States is averse to domesticating international values and norms on greenhouse gas emissions, the death penalty, landmines, the pursuit of universal justice, etc. But this self-image of exceptionalism is neither congruent with how others see it nor conducive to securing the cooperation of others.

Contrary to some instant explanations offered after 9/11 that the United States is the terrorists' target of choice because of its success, dynamism and openness, the core basis of international respect for the American Republic, albeit with reservations and caveats, is its extraordinary success as a society, economy and polity. The UN Charter articulates quintessentially US values. In truth the peace of the world since 1945 has depended more on US power and wisdom than UN felicity. The US commitment to the post-1945 order had emphasized the protection of the democratic community through rules constraining the use of force by "the other side"; the impact of 9/11 in the moment of unipolar triumph saw an expansion in the use of force to promote and export the democratic franchise. The naive enthusiasm has waned since.

Imperialism is not a foreign policy designed to promote, project and globalize the values and virtues of the dominant centre, but a form of international governance based on an unequal hierarchy of power. The reality of inequality structures the relationship between the imperial centre and all others. This is not a matter of malevolence on the part of a particular administration in Washington, but an artefact of the reality of a unipolar world that will shape the foreign relations of any administration. All sides must learn to live with this reality.

Nevertheless, progress towards the good international society requires that force be harnessed to authority. The United Nations has authority but no power. It seeks to replace the balance of power with a community of power. The United States has global power and reach but lacks international authority. The United Nations, universal in membership, symbolizes global governance but lacks the attributes of international government. The United States often acts – has no choice but to act – as a de facto world government, but disclaims responsibility for the distributional outcomes of its actions with regard to resources, environment, labour and justice.

Just as the United States is a nation of laws, so the United Nations is dedicated to establishing the rule of international law. The UN Charter was a triumph of hope and idealism over the experience of two world wars. The flame of idealism flickers when buffeted by passing storms, but refuses to die out. In the midst of the swirling tides of change, the United Nations is still the symbol of our dreams for a better world, where weakness can be compensated by justice and fairness, and the law of the jungle replaced by the rule of law. History's learning curve shows that the UN ideal can neither be fully attained nor ever abandoned.

The United Nations remains our one and best hope for unity of purpose and action in a world of almost infinite diversity – a world in which problems without passports require solutions without passports. Unbridled nationalism and the raw interplay of power must be mediated and moderated in its international framework. Of course the United Nations is an international bureaucracy with many failings and flaws; and a forum often used and abused by governments for finger pointing, not problem solving. Too often has the United Nations demonstrated a failure to tackle urgent collective action problems due to institutionalized inability, incapacity or unwillingness. These are the three facets – an international bureaucracy, a politicians' talkshop and a spineless-toothless cop on the beat – that draw the most trenchant criticism.

Yet the United Nations remains the focus of international expectations and the locus of collective action. The reason for this is that more, much more, than the attributes of bureaucratic rigidity, institutional timidity and intergovernmental trench warfare, the United Nations is the one body that houses the divided fragments of humanity. It is an idea, a symbol of an imagined and constructed community of strangers. It exists to bring about a world where fear is changed to hope, want gives way to dignity, and apprehensions are turned into aspirations.

51

Crying wolf diminished the West's credibility

The Canberra Times, 24 May 2006

Those in favour of the Iraq war option back in 2003 tended to dismiss doubters as wimps. Curiously, their courage fails them in a frank and honest assessment today of the consequences of their past choices. The Iraq war's legacy includes diminished Western credibility in highlighting an Iran threat, narrower policy options in responding to the nuclear challenge and an Iran that is simultaneously politically stronger in Iraq, richer because of rising oil prices and more emboldened and motivated on national security.

The United Nations, built to preserve peace, is not a pacifist organization. It was created on the fundamental premise that sometimes force would indeed have to be used, even to defend peace, against international outlaws. It has not always done so, and so peace has had to depend much more on US power than UN authority.

But the abiding lesson is that if force is used unwisely, prematurely or recklessly, the possibility of its use plummets when it is both necessary and fully justified. In the end this is the most damning indictment of those who entangled us in the Iraq misadventure: that it distracted attention from the real threats and dangers, sapped the will, corroded the capacity to confront genuine challenges and emboldened those who might otherwise have remained more cautious to become more brazen.

Taking a country to war is among the most solemn responsibilities that a government has. First because it puts one's soldiers at risk of death and injury, second because it asks one's soldiers to kill complete strangers on government orders, third because it kills many civilians caught in the crossfire, and fourth because the immediate and long-term consequences are both very grave and quite unpredictable.

The stated justification for the Iraq war was the threat of weapons of mass destruction in the hands of Saddam Hussein. It is not for those who oppose war to prove their case, but for proponents to prove it beyond reasonable doubt. Having cried wolf – more accurately, having been caught out crying wolf – should leaders complain about a ho-hum response to the newest dire warnings of the same threat?

To argue that the real reason for the war was the brutality of Saddam is to say that on this most solemn international responsibility, governments should be allowed to lie to their people. I will gladly admit to dissenting from this, always.

Al-Qaeda and their fundamentalist fellow-travellers were on the run, badly demoralized and universally stigmatized after 9/11 and the internationally supported war in Afghanistan. Iraq fragmented their enemies' military and political efforts, ensnared the United States in a military and diplomatic quagmire, regained sympathy to their cause and fresh recruits to their ranks, renewed their sense of mission and purpose and generally turned a strategic setback into a fresh opportunity. Now even the Afghanistan mission is being questioned.

History shows that democracies are reluctant to fight. But if forced into wars, democratic governments that have the support of their people tend to prevail, making them "powerful pacifists." Iraq has increased citizens' suspicions of their own governments and badly fractured domestic opinion in the countries that went to war. This handicaps them from considering another war, even when there is a clear and present danger to national and international security.

The biggest external political victor of the continuing developments in Iraq is Iran, riding on the coat-tails of the Iraqi Shiite majority and Shiite militia. Given its strategic location between them, and its vast population, Iran could make life vastly more interesting for foreigners in both Afghanistan and Iraq.

Conversely, with nuclear neighbours to its west, north and east, and large numbers of American military forces all around it, what is a prudent national security planner to recommend to the Iranian government? To abandon or accelerate the nuclear programme if one exists? In going to war against Iraq, a major argument was that in the international jungle, international law, if there is such a thing, cannot trump national security. Countries have to rely on their military might to avoid becoming the victims of others.

Where we lead, will they not follow?

In the meantime, the escalating price of oil, fuelled by the continuing Iraq insurgency and resulting interruptions of oil production and supply

with fears of further shortages, has swelled Iranian coffers and strengthened their bargaining position against threats of international sanctions.

The political cost of a military option against yet another Islamic country will be much higher because of Iraq.

All of which might put the ball firmly back in the United Nations'
court. But has the United Nations' authority been enhanced or diminished by the Iraq war? An organization brushed aside as irrelevant in
one crisis cannot simply be lifted out of the rubbish bin of history and
dusted off for use in another.

52

It's time, now, to end the travesty that is Guantanamo Bay

The Canberra Times, 11 July 2006

The long detention without trial of David Hicks is a small but sad metaphor of how the so-called war on terror lost its moral compass. Australia's failure to demand justice for him is an abdication of the government's responsibility to protect its citizens. The whole sorry saga is
wrong in law, lacking in moral integrity and bad politics to boot.

Perversely, the whole point of Guantanamo Bay in Cuba was to take
prisoners outside the protection of any legal regime. Even the British
law justice Johan Steyn described it, already in November 2003, as a "legal black hole" that was "a stain on United States justice." The administration's doctrine amounts to the right of the US military to hold people
indefinitely without trial in an undeclared and never-ending war against
unnamed enemies.

Two separate issues became merged in the public debate: the relevant
legal regime that should apply to prisoners in this particular war, and
abuses in the actual treatment of the prisoners. The designation of prisoners as "enemy combatants" and their confinement and treatment in
Guantanamo raised serious questions about the US commitment to fair
trials and impartial justice. The abused accounted for a minority of prisoners held by the United States, but they were integral to the war: they
provided the standard of terrorism by which the good behaviour of the
rest would be judged and enforced.

Still, the robustness and resilience of the US commitment to human
rights laws and norms will be judged in the final analysis not by the
breaches in the aftermath of 9/11, but by the reversal and attenuation of

the breaches through domestic judicial and political processes as well as the pressures of civil society. The unlawfulness of the charade of justice at Guantanamo, long argued by many eminent international lawyers, has been confirmed by the US Supreme Court. It has also affirmed the applicability of the Geneva Conventions.

Second, Guantanamo flouts not just due process, but also common decency and basic morality. The rise and diffusion of human rights norms and conventions and the extension and diffusion of international humanitarian law were among the truly great achievements of the last century. Guantanamo represents a serious setback to this progressive development.

A human right, owed to every person simply as a human being, is inherently universal. Held only by human beings, but equally by all, it does not flow from any office, rank or relationship. The language of human rights embodies the intuition that the human species is one and every individual is entitled to equal moral consideration.

Amnesty International's secretary-general Irene Khan wrote last year that, "The detention facility at Guantanamo Bay has become the gulag of our times, entrenching the practice of arbitrary and indefinite detention in violation of international law. Trials by military commissions have made a mockery of justice and due process." She added that, "When the most powerful country in the world thumbs its nose at the rule of law and human rights, it grants a licence to others to commit abuse with impunity." The gulag analogy may be a hyperbole – but that is cold comfort to those of us who believe in America, believe that it should hold to a higher standard than "we're better than the gulag."

UN Security Council Resolution 1456 (20 January 2003) imposes an obligation on all states to ensure that counter-terrorism measures comply with international human rights, refugees and international humanitarian law obligations. The prohibition of torture appears on every short list of universal standards of human behaviour. The debate on whether under some circumstances torture can be justified if it leads to preventing mass terrorist attacks mirrors long-argued positions on cultural relativism. A posture of moral relativism can be profoundly racist, proclaiming in effect that "the other" is not worthy of the dignity that belongs inalienably to one.

By contrast, human rights advocacy rests, in Michael Ignatieff's words, on "the moral imagination to feel the pain of others" as our own. It treats others as "rights-bearing equals" and can be considered as "a juridical articulation of duty by those in zones of safety towards those in zones of danger." It is vividly captured in the World War II joke that they came after the workers; I was not a worker, so I did not object. They came after the homosexuals; I wasn't one, so I did not object. They came after the Jews; I wasn't one, so I did not object. Then they came after me. There was no one left to object.

If not me, it could be my son in David Hicks's predicament. I want my government to privilege its obligations to protect the lives and defend the rights of Australians over the politics of alliance solidarity or subservience to a foreign power.

Finally, it is bad politics. The New York-based Human Rights Watch argues that abuses committed by the United States in Guantanamo (and Iraq) significantly weaken the world's ability to protect human rights. When a country as dominant as the United States openly flouts the law, it tempts others to mimic its policy. It also reduces US leverage over others, since it cannot call on others to uphold principles it itself violates.

Guantanamo is a shorthand for the hypocrisy and moral bankruptcy of a war that was meant to defend our values against assault from the lawless barbarians. As such it has been among the more effective rallying cries and recruiting drives for the jihadists. As the conditions of detention of suspected foreign terrorists in Guantanamo became widely known in the Muslim world, they contributed to a hardening of the jihad through shahid (martyrdom). Nasra Hassan's study of the phenomenon of suicide terrorism, published in the *Atlantic Monthly* in June 2004, documents the belief among many Muslim youth that "death is preferable to Guantanamo Bay."

So: charge David Hicks, or bring him home. If he has committed crimes, let him have his day in court, and pay the price if convicted. If not, if he was merely a delusional and lost kid, let him go.

53

Don't be too easily appeased

The Australian, 13 July 2006

Almost 200 killed and another 500 wounded. India's financial capital brought to its knees. A nation in shock and grief.

The world shares the pain, anger and determination to face down the bastards, not to give them the triumph of being cowed down or the satisfaction of fomenting communal hatred and bloodletting. For security from acts and the fear of terrorism is indeed indivisible, and the world is the battlefield.

We have been here before. In 1993, twin attacks on the financial centre and Air India building proved to be dress rehearsals for 9/11 in New York. The world ignored then how India and Southwest Asia had joined the frontline of global terrorism. No longer.

The most immediate tasks will be to help the victims, tighten security throughout India to forestall further attacks, probe and plug the fatal gaps in intelligence that made this possible and prevent outbreaks of violence against Muslims. Bombay (now Mumbai) was back to normal within 24 hours in 1993; it can do so again.

The chances are high that the perpetrators will turn out to have pan-Islamic links with the banned Students Islamic Movement of India, or similar groups in Pakistan and Bangladesh.

However, not all Muslims are terrorists and not all terrorists are Muslim. Before the Iraq war, the leading practitioners of suicide terrorism were Sri Lanka's Tamil Tigers: Hindus. The most ruthless terrorism in India in the 1980s was perpetrated by Sikhs. Europe, including Britain, has had its share of Christian terrorists. If anything, India's 140 million

Muslims are a salutary negation of the facile thesis about Islam's incompatibility with democracy. If India abandoned secularism, and if the localized and sporadic killings of Muslims by Hindu lynch mobs, as in Gujarat, became general and widespread, the country would be convulsed and destroyed.

In a one billion-strong country with an 80 per cent Hindu population, the prime minister and army chief are Sikhs, the president is a Muslim and the power behind the throne is an Italian-origin Catholic: profound testimony to the pluralism and accommodation of India's complex but adaptable power-sharing arrangements. Democratic politics, political freedoms, civil liberties and religious tolerance must be protected at all costs.

But India has earned its reputation as a soft state that can be intimidated into meeting terrorists' demands.

The best exemplars are the United States and Israel: no negotiation with terrorists, period.

As well as being tough on terrorists, India needs to be tough on the causes of terrorism. Poverty is not a direct cause but is an incubator of terrorism and a root cause of corruption. New Delhi needs to be tough on implementing reforms to maintain rapid economic growth. Another tough measure is solving long-running territorial conflicts. More than 90 per cent of suicide terrorists aim at compelling military forces to withdraw from territory they view as their homeland under foreign occupation.

India's terrorism problem today is specific to Kashmir, not generic to Muslims. The obvious, and probably only, solution is to make the Line of Control the international border. Neither Islamabad nor New Delhi has had the courage for this, nor outsiders the courage to insist on it.

External involvement in Kashmiri militancy is not absent. The world must persuade, coax or coerce regimes that are tolerant of export-only terrorist cells to confront the menace instead. One group's terrorist can no longer be tolerated as another's freedom fighter.

The blowback phenomenon has returned to haunt the West from supporting jihad against Soviet-occupied Afghanistan. It consumed Indira (Sikhs) and Rajiv (Tamils) Gandhi. Pakistan remains in danger of tearing itself apart from the inside because of armed elements espousing a variety of foreign extremist causes. South Asian neighbours must pool resources to root out the tyranny of terrorism throughout the region.

Finally, India must address the corruption and politicization of the police forces and the dreadfully antiquated standards of their training, equipment and discipline, as well as the criminalization of politics. The number of state and federal parliamentarians with pending criminal cases is alarming. Terrorism will thrive in such conditions.

54

Containing chemical weapons

The Japan Times, 24 July 2006

Recent events from the Middle East to Northeast Asia have once again highlighted the unsatisfactory state of affairs with respect to the tool kit available to the international community for responding to the challenge of weapons of mass destruction. This makes it all the more curious as to why more attention is not paid to the one area where success is more clearly demonstrable.

Chemical, biological and nuclear weapons can inflict mass casualties in a single attack. The first two have been outlawed. The Chemical Weapons Convention (CWC), in force since 1997, is the jewel in the crown of global treaties regulating weapons of mass destruction (WMD).

Unlike the more familiar Nuclear Non-Proliferation Treaty (NPT), the CWC is universal and does not create a world of chemical apartheid in which a small group of countries is in legitimate possession of weapons that are banned for all others. Unlike the Biological Weapons Convention (BWC), the CWC contains rigorous provisions on monitoring and verification that routinely reach into the private sector to a depth and breadth neither contemplated before nor emulated since. Universality, equality, nondiscrimination and the promise of effectiveness have helped secure near-total adherence to the CWC, embracing 95 and 98 percent of the world's population and chemical industry respectively.

The use of chemicals as weapons – poisoned arrows, arsenic smoke, noxious fumes – is as old as human history. Their range, accuracy and lethality increased exponentially with the efficient harnessing for large-scale deployment, utilizing modern industrial processes and organization.

There has been a matching interest in limiting the use of chemicals as tools of war. The CWC was the product of 20 years' negotiations for a treaty-based ban on the production, possession, proliferation, transfer and use of chemical weapons, and their total elimination. It is the only multilateral treaty to ban an entire category of WMD, provide for international verification of their destruction and the conversion of their production facilities to peaceful purposes, and actively involve the global chemicals industry in treaty negotiations and ongoing verification. The CWC also promotes international cooperation in the peaceful uses of chemicals and provides for assistance and protection to countries under chemical weapons (CW) threat or attack.

The convention requires destruction of all declared CW arsenals and production facilities. Unlike the NPT and the BWC, it establishes an implementing secretariat. The Organization for the Prohibition of Chemical Weapons (OPCW) is required to oversee and verify the total destruction of all declared chemical weapons; inactivate and destroy or convert to peaceful purposes all CW production facilities; and inspect the production and, in some cases, the processing and consumption of dual-use chemicals, and receive declarations of their transfer, in order to ensure their exclusive peaceful use.

The OPCW membership totals 186 countries. It has developed a database of over 1,500 CW-related compounds. It works also to improve our capacity to respond to chemical attack and protect civilian populations.

All declared CW production capacity has been inactivated, with 55 of the 65 CW production facilities certified as destroyed or converted to peaceful purposes. Inventory of all declared CW stockpiles has been completed, though only 2.5 million of the 8.7 million munitions have been destroyed. Just a tiny drop of nerve agent the size of a pinhead can kill an adult within minutes, yet only under 14,000 of the 71,000 tons of declared CW agents have been destroyed. Over 6,000 industrial facilities around the world are liable for inspection.

Although the "architecture" for banning chemical weapons is complete and effective, many critical components of the inspections regime remain untested, and efforts are in train for achieving universality, reporting of dual-use exports and imports, and ensuring effective verification and enforcement. With the verified destruction of only one-fifth of declared weapons agents, the goal of destruction of all CW stockpiles by the agreed extended deadline of 2012 may not be met.

The OPCW has conducted 2,500 inspections at 200 military and 700 industrial sites in 76 countries. But it is yet to refer a case of possible non-compliance to the UN Security Council. This curious oddity, of a distinctively strong challenge inspection system that has never been utilized, may indicate that the convention's deterrent effect has been perfect. But the effectiveness of a system yet to be tested must remain under question.

Is the CWC a dinosaur, a relic left over from the Cold War? Or a model for multilateral undertakings to build global consensus on security through arms control, create confidence and deter treaty violations? The international challenge inspection system is reinforced by national legislation and measures on criminalization of proliferation activities, effective protection of proliferation sensitive personnel, materials and equipment, control and accounting systems for monitoring materials and stocks, and regulation and surveillance of dual-use transfers.

In these respects, the OPCW shows the way for the NPT and the BWC in addressing proliferation threats. But it must continually adapt to an evolving situation where chemical weapons are part of the bigger picture of possible use of hazardous materials by terrorists and criminal organizations. The challenge is as real as the stakes are high.

55

What passing bells for those who die as UN peacekeepers?

The Hindu, 3 August 2006

In 1999, I organized and chaired a workshop in Budapest on the fallout and longer-term implications of the Kosovo war. I asked retired Air Marshal Ray Funnel, chief of the Australian Air Force during Gulf War I in 1991, to address the question whether this was the first war to be won by air power. ("With respect, professor," he said, "that's a stupid question." But that's another story.) During the question and answer session, someone asked him whether the NATO bombing of the Chinese embassy in Belgrade was deliberate or accidental.

"With all the authority I have as an air force officer," Air Marshal Funnel replied, "let me assure you that there is no way that bombing could have been deliberate. The American military just doesn't operate like that, and that would have been too stupid an act to be a deliberate decision."

Another participant in the project was Lt. Gen. Satish Nambiar, former deputy chief of the Indian Army and the first commanding officer of the UN Protection Force in the former Yugoslavia. He countered (to vigorous nodding assent from our Chinese participant) that "With all the authority I have as a retired army general and someone who knows Belgrade quite well, let me tell you there is no way that the hit on the Chinese Embassy could have been accidental."

The seeming contradiction is in fact resolvable. For both statements to be true, the strike was not due to a high-level policy decision in Washington, nor an example of "stuff happens," but an operational decision by a lower level "rogue" field commander or targeting officer.

Similarly, from everything I know and believe about Israel, it is inconceivable that the UN post was targeted as a matter of deliberate policy. But from all that is already known, it seems equally implausible that deaths were caused merely by an accidental strike or operational error. Official Israeli policy will be judged by the punishment meted out to those responsible for the atrocity.

The UN position in Khiyyam has been well known to the Israeli Defence Force (IDF) for many years and was clearly marked. The Israelis had given assurances that the UN posts and personnel would not be struck. On 18 July, UN monitors made 10 phone calls between 1:20 p.m., when an Israeli plane dropped a bomb 300 metres from the patrol base, and around 7:17 p.m. Lt. Col. John Molloy, the senior Irish peacekeeper in Lebanon and a key liaison officer with the IDF, gave six warnings about the Khiyyam post that were "very specific, explicit, detailed and stark." In New York, UN Assistant Secretary-General Jane Lute phoned the Israeli mission, and then appealed to Deputy Secretary-General Mark Malloch Brown to follow suit, reiterating protests and calling for an end to artillery shelling and aerial bombardments.

After the hit on Khiyyam, the United Nations secured IDF agreement for safe passage for two of its armoured personnel carriers which arrived around 9:30 p.m. but were attacked by Israel. Israel also fired on peacekeepers sent to dig out the bodies. Ireland's Foreign Minister Dermot Ahern remarked that the incident "raises questions about whether this was an accident."

Lightly armed UN peacekeeping forces are not meant to stand up to and resist an Israeli military incursion across the international border. Their central purpose is to give effect to a pacific intent, not to check a war of choice. This makes them easy targets. By the end of 2005, a total of 2,227 personnel had died while serving in UN peacekeeping operations, some in accidents, others killed on duty. They sacrificed their lives for a cause above and beyond even national defence, for an abstract principle of international duty. There is no higher calling nor nobler cause.

With apologies to Wilfred Owen, what passing bells for those who die as UN peacekeepers – only the monstrous silence of the disunited nations? In response to the death of three of its soldiers killed and the kidnapping of two, Israel unleashed an orgy of destruction and cruelty whose victims have overwhelmingly been civilians caught in the crossfire.

In response to four unarmed and neutral UN peacekeepers being killed by Israel, against the background of repeated pleas over six hours to stop before a tragedy occurred, Kofi Annan denounced this "apparently deliberate targeting" of the UN post. Would I want as my secretary-general someone who is complicit through silence when his own peacekeepers are killed? He can soften and back-pedal subsequently, but I for one am glad he spoke up when he did.

When some Western leaders and editorialists shift the blame for the death of UN observers to Hezbollah and the United Nations, on the twisted reasoning that the United Nations should have withdrawn them from a war zone, they are effectively outsourcing the setting of their international moral compass to Israel. As Israel encounters stiffer than expected resistance and world outrage and condemnation rises of the mounting human toll, calls grow for a ceasefire followed by the deployment of a fresh peacekeeping force. The nature and prospects of a new mission will depend crucially on whether it is conceived and designed as a force to reward or punish Israel for its aggression, or disarm Hezbollah and stop it from attacking Israel.

Israel's UN ambassador is publicly contemptuous of the current UN Interim Force in Lebanon. He mockingly notes that "Interim in UN jargon is 28 years." His condescension betrays an ignorance of history. The United Nations had been extremely reluctant to establish a peacekeeping force in the aftermath of Israel's 1978 invasion of southern Lebanon. It succumbed to US pressure because Washington wanted to rescue Israel from the ill-advised invasion, but inserted the word "interim" in the name as a compromise. The force has been renewed every six months partly because of the reluctance to admit failure, partly to prevent Israel from reaping the fruits of aggression, and partly because the force has performed many functions of a *de facto* local municipal authority and overseen a repopulation of the region under its stabilizing auspices.

The open Israeli contempt for UN peacekeeping and the deaths of unarmed international observers will make countries much more reluctant to contribute to a bolstered or replacement UN force. Having privileged its historic role as the ultimate guarantor of Israel's security over the minimum degree of impartiality required to play an honest broker role, can the United States organize a multinational peacekeeping force?

Any US-led or NATO force would be seen, resented, and resisted as Israel's instrument. The United States and its coalition of the dwindling are tied down in an increasingly lethal civil war in Iraq whose daily average civilian death toll has reached 100. The Taliban is resurgent in Afghanistan, challenging NATO forces across increasingly expanding areas of the country. Enlarging the theatre of conflict to Lebanon will merely confirm many Muslims' suspicions of NATO as the armed wing of the Christian West against the rest.

Sadly, it may be futile to expect significant progress on resolving the Middle East conflicts until a prior exorcism of the historical guilt over the Holocaust by the West, which explains their lack of balance.

56

Intelligence works better than bullets

The Japan Times, 16 August 2006

The British police, acting closely with intelligence agencies in the United States, Pakistan and perhaps elsewhere over many months, have foiled a major terrorist plot of blowing up numerous planes between Britain and America.

Western observers are pleased and relieved that the planned mass murder has been thwarted by vigilant law-enforcement authorities. But the hardline reaction of some, who take this as vindication of the "tough" policies of London and Washington (not to mention Israel), and proof of the naivete and error of liberals' talk about "root causes" of terrorism, is enough to make one despair.

Dealing with terrorism requires hard-nosed analysis followed by an equally hard-nosed multipronged policy: apprehending and punishing those who commit terrorism; preventing acts of terrorism; reducing the numbers of terrorists; weakening their motivation; and softening support for them in their communities. Instead we get rhetoric on steroids.

There is unanimous support for the first two tasks but disagreement over the rest. The old balance between liberty, due process and security may have to be re-examined and readjusted – but not abandoned, for then indeed the terrorists will have won in destroying our values and freedoms. The British success is vindication of the approach that emphasizes law enforcement and criminalization over military warfare and detention without trial. Putting arrested suspects on trial, presenting compelling evidence of guilt and securing a criminal conviction will avoid suspicions of group-directed vendetta and force British Muslims to confront the reality of the evil in their midst.

But thwarting some planned attacks through clever detection will not, of itself, stop the numbers of terrorists from multiplying, their motivation to carry out mass carnage from strengthening, or in-community support for them from firming and increasing. The equation is quite simple: Are we, the good guys, capturing, killing, deterring and dissuading more would-be terrorists than they, the bad guys, are recruiting, training and deploying? Do our actions, statements and policies increase or diminish sympathy, support and incentives for them?

The difference between terrorism and criminality lies mainly in the political motivation: the desire to change politics through violence targeted at civilians. In addition to, but not as a substitute for, tough criminal law enforcement, therefore, we need to address the political causes. More terrorists have been spawned by outsiders occupying their territory than by any other cause. The Iraq and Lebanon wars are likely to multiply terrorists by spawning a new generation of battle-hardened jihadists. The occupation of Iraq played into the hands of US enemies ideologically, tactically and strategically. It incited a deep hatred of US foreign policy around the world in general and among Muslims in particular. There was no al-Qaeda in Iraq before the arrival of Western troops. It became a terrorist swamp because of the war.

Between them, Iraq and Lebanon will lead many more to sympathize with and support radical jihadists willing to kill Westerners. Again, the equation is remarkably simple: If we kill one terrorist in a strike on a house that also has 100 civilians, of whom 10 survivors or relatives of those killed join the terrorists, we have gone nine steps backward.

More people today than on 9/11 view the United States as a major threat. In a 15-nation poll in June, more people in more countries considered the United States to be a greater danger to world peace than Iran's nuclear ambitions. In another poll, 36 per cent of Europeans identified the United States as the greatest threat to world stability.

Iraq and Lebanon are devastated and Islamist forces are strengthening. Iran is more empowered, enriched and emboldened. Washington is unable to engage Syria and Iran, which have influence over Hezbollah and Iraq's Shiites. US allies in the region have little credibility with Arab opinion, their legitimacy with their own people is suspect and their pro-US policies help to promote the growth of militant Islamists.

Peter Bouckaert, emergencies director of the New York-based Human Rights Watch, reports that Israel has repeatedly hit civilian homes and cars, killing dozens of people, with no evidence of any military objective. Rather, "Israel is prefabricating excuses to justify killing civilians." Incidentally, he was the investigator who debunked widely reported allegations of Israeli massacres in Jenin in 2002: hardly a stereotypical anti-Semite.

US and British backing of Israel's military offensive and resistance to calls for an immediate ceasefire will give a new generation of angry and vengeful Arabs and Muslims a renewed mission and cause against Israel and the West.

Hezbollah is a terrorist organization, but its proven resistance to Israel has galvanized the Arab street, united the Arab and Islamic worlds and, in Hassan Nasrullah, produced the first pan-Arab hero since Gamel Abdul Nasser in 1956. Even with victories in sporadic battles like the London plot, the war on terror may be getting longer. The correct, British, approach is through intelligence that apprehends wannabe terrorists with pinpoint precision: no bombs, no invasions, no one killed. The other approach is through scattershot attacks that kill many civilians in unnecessary wars and add to the lengthening line of jihadists. It is not possible to delegitimize terrorism while killing many civilians in endless wars.

57

Lebanon war: An exercise in futility

The Daily Yomiuri, 29 August 2006

A thousand killed, a million displaced and infrastructure gutted: this is akin to what the rampaging militias did in East Timor in 1999. How do we impress on war-inflamed consciousness the great gulf between the goals sought, the price paid and the results gained?

International law governs when force may be used; international humanitarian law governs how force may be used. Even in self-defence, the use of force is still subject to significant limitations of scale, duration, intensity and targets. Even when justified and justly waged, it may produce bad results.

Israel said its actions were a legitimate response to relentless Hezbollah attacks. The right of self-defence is well-established and universally acknowledged. After 9/11, UN Security Council Resolution 1368 explicitly incorporated acts against terrorism into the right of self-defence.

The right to resist foreign occupation is also well-established. Part of the intractability of the Middle East conflict lies in this difference. One side defines freedom in opposition to terrorism, the other in opposition to foreign occupation.

Nothing justifies terrorism as a tactic. The Palestinians may have a just cause and a justified grievance. But blowing up a busload of schoolchildren is still an act of terrorism, not a battle in an armed liberation struggle. The violation of the civilian immunity principle by suicide bombers has been a political catastrophe for the Palestinian cause. Similarly, Hezbollah rocket attacks, which target towns as they cannot be aimed with any precision at military targets, are indiscriminate, illegal and illegitimate.

Secondly, with an agnostic attitude about who was to blame for war and unequivocal condemnation of terrorism, one can still be highly critical of how civilians were the chief casualties of Israel's war.

Israel puts the blame for the high civilian toll on Hezbollah, for deliberately shielding and hiding fighters and rockets amidst civilians. Is the claim factually true? If so, can the moral blame be shifted from the perpetrator to the intended target of the violence?

The claim that high civilian casualties resulted from Hezbollah hiding its fighters and weapons among them was unquestioningly accepted by many Western journalists. They gave more face-value credence to Israeli government statements than they do normally to their own.

Yet the claim is suspect. Independent accounts failed to corroborate the charge that Hezbollah deliberately used civilians as shields to protect them from retaliatory Israeli attack. They did sometimes store weapons in or near civilian homes and UN observers, which are serious violations of the laws of war.

Human Rights Watch, whose investigations debunked widely believed allegations of Israeli massacres in Jenin in 2002, concluded that at best, Israel had blurred the distinction between civilian and combatant. At worst, the "pattern of attacks" suggests that "the failures cannot be explained or dismissed as mere accidents; the extent of the pattern and the seriousness of the consequences indicate the commission of war crimes." Amnesty International has just published a report (Wednesday) that comes to substantially the same conclusion.

Thirdly, even if justified, legitimate and proportionate, war may still prove foolish. Like Iraq for the United States, a war that was meant to showcase awesome and unchallengeable military might has proven instead the military limits of the regional superpower. It has crippled and weakened Lebanon, enlarging the political space that Hezbollah can capture, and strengthened its popularity and appeal among Arabs and Muslims.

Hezbollah seriously miscalculated the ferocity of the Israeli response to provocations. Israel badly overestimated its own military prowess and underestimated Hezbollah's arsenal, skills and resilience as a fighting force. On the Arab street there is intensified hatred for Israel and the United States (which blocked calls for an immediate ceasefire and urgently resupplied the Israeli military in the meantime), contempt for corrupt and autocratic Arab regimes and support for Hezbollah.

What if, after some time and sobering introspection, Lebanese come to believe that Hezbollah is responsible for provoking fierce Israeli attacks:

will it still be seen as a protector against rather than a provoker of Israeli aggression?

A month after hostilities began – the delay caused open dismay and distress to UN Secretary-General Kofi Annan – the Security Council unanimously approved Resolution 1701 on 12 August. Power equations in the Security Council prevailed. Its three overarching goals are to secure Israel's vulnerable northern border, strengthen the Lebanese government and contain Hezbollah.

Ignoring the long, tortured, tit-for-tat history of the Israel-Arab conflict, the resolution demands "immediate cessation" of Hezbollah attacks but only of "offensive" Israeli operations – presumably as judged unilaterally by Israel. This has already proven a weak point with an Israeli commando raid into Lebanon since the ceasefire.

Other countries are prohibited from supplying "any entity or individual in Lebanon" arms or training in the use of arms. This is a classic triumph of hope over experience.

Israel is not required to pay any reparation for the damage inflicted on Lebanon's infrastructure. Its public statements indicate a clear understanding that the UN force will do Israel's work vis-a-vis Hezbollah.

If Hezbollah perceives the resolution as one-sided and unjust, it will refuse to comply. What then? The size of the UN Interim Force in Lebanon (UNIFIL) is to be bolstered to 15,000, and its mandate made more robust: it is authorized "to take all necessary action" in its area of operations. Can UNIFIL forcibly defeat and disarm Hezbollah when Israel signally failed to do so? The biggest long-term danger for the United Nations is that its reputation as a front organization for the United States, useful in furtherance of US interest but disposable otherwise, could be cemented in many Muslim minds, thereby seriously eroding its legitimacy – its only real asset.

The United Nations' reputation could be salvaged by taking the lead in reaching a comprehensive peace settlement. The core of any deal will draw on existing plans and resolutions: the return of Israel from captured and occupied territories to the 1967 borders, roughly rather than precisely; the creation of a Palestinian state alongside Israel; a solution to the refugee problem which does not lead to a general right of return; a solution to the status of the holy places; and full recognition of Israel from Arabs and a peaceful coexistence.

58

Both sides must learn compromise if Lebanon is to survive intact

The Canberra Times, 11 September 2006

In the 1980s I taught the introductory course in international relations at Otago University. I used to discuss such perennial problems as Kashmir and Palestine. I would outline two models, and ask the students to pick which was more likely to lead to resolution and which to perpetuation of the conflicts.

Model 1 assumes that in any dispute there are at least two parties who disagree over facts, causes, consequences and the best way forward. Both sides are wrong, neither being entirely blameless. Both will have to live with each other, no matter how the conflict ends. This will be easier if both sides compromise, with mutual give-and-take and accommodation.

Model 2 holds one side as totally right and the other wrong. The virtuous should not negotiate with evil but destroy it. Principles are not for sale, cannot be bargained away and must never be compromised. History proves that appeasement merely whets the appetite of the aggressor, not buy lasting peace.

Almost all students identified the interest-based Model 1 as likely to resolve and the value-based Model 2 as likely to prolong conflicts. I then asked them to apply the reasoning to the Australia, New Zealand and United States of America (ANZUS) security treaty dispute with the United States over nuclear warships. The classroom consensus collapsed in a chorus of "buts" that would have done a smokers' convention proud.

I am reminded of that by reactions to the commentary in the Western press critical of Israel's Lebanon war.

A body of research shows that with our own actions, we tend to re-member the cause – why we did it, which provides a rational explanation for our behaviour.

For opponents, the why is ignored and forgotten. Instead we remem-ber what they did and the damaging consequences for us. The memory festers as a lingering grievance.

To say that both sides must share blame in any conflict does not imply that both are equally to blame. Even if Israel faces existential threats, does it profit them to be judged by the standard of terrorists: we are no worse than our enemies?

Emergencies director of the New York-based Human Rights Watch Peter Bouckaert investigated a number of Israeli strikes on civilian tar-gets. He concluded that "time after time," Israel "hit civilian homes and cars in the southern border zone, killing dozens of people with no evi-dence of any military objective." Consequently, "Israel's claims about pinpoint strikes and proportionate responses are pure fantasy."

UN Secretary-General Kofi Annan, too, placed the attack on Qana in the context of "a pattern of violations of international law, including in-ternational humanitarian law and international human rights law, com-mitted during the current hostilities."

Isolated and occasional operational errors and accidental mistakes are one thing; a systematic pattern suggests possible war crimes. An indepen-dent investigation by Amnesty International concluded that strikes on ci-vilian infrastructure were an integral part of Israel's military strategy. Amnesty therefore called for an urgent, comprehensive and independent UN inquiry into grave violations of international humanitarian law by both Hezbollah and Israel.

The UN's humanitarian chief, Jan Egeland, of Norway, condemned the intensified use of cluster bombs by Israel in the last 72 hours of the war – as the deadline for the ceasefire approached – as "completely immoral." With some 100,000 unexploded cluster bombs strewn about southern Lebanon, every day people are being "maimed, wounded and killed," he said.

These are not the usual suspects of anti-Israeli individuals and institu-tions, but people normally very sympathetic to Israel's predicament of living in a harsh and hostile environment.

It is easy to attack opponents and tempting to try to discredit critics. It requires moral courage to look in the mirror for faults. Yet this might actually prove more productive to solving a conflict instead of perpetuat-ing it for decades.

I have been called a traitor to India and attacked for promoting India's agenda as a UN official; attacked for being anti-American and a career apologist for US foreign policy (by the late David Lange when New Zealand's prime minister, no less); denounced for anti-Semitism and promoting closer India-Israel relations at the cost of India's domestic Muslim population and foreign relations with the large group of Islamic countries; and condemned for being an apologist for Palestinian terrorism and for Israeli-US aggression. Life would be dull if peace broke out.

.Some Israeli and diaspora Jews have spoken out on Lebanon. Thus Oxford's Avi Shlaim: "Killing children is wrong. Period. A 'war on terror' cannot be won by a democratically elected government acting like a terrorist organization." Rabbi David Goldberg: "by creating a wilderness in Lebanon and calling it peace, Israel has recruited thousands of new martyrs to the Hezbollah cause." American Norman Birnbaum regrets "the transformation of a significant group of Jewish commentators, intellectuals and scholars from critical advocates of universal values into apologists for US moral superiority and global domination."

Former Israeli military officer Avi Azrieli notes "Israel is the most dangerous place in the world for Jews today" – an ironic outcome for a Zionist movement that sought to establish in Israel a safe haven from murderous anti-Semitism.

In another irony, the Jewish state was established to protect the diaspora, but now the diaspora works to protect Israel. To reverse this, Israel must come to terms with its Middle Eastern identity and location and shift "from survival by intimidation and isolation to accommodation and dialogue," Azrieli says.

Does this mean Israel is the sole or primary culprit in the endless cycle of Middle East violence? Of course not. The country and the people retain, rightly, a large reservoir of goodwill in Western society. But the goodwill is neither uncritical nor inexhaustible.

59

North Korea & envisioning alternative nuclear futures

The Hindu, 11 October 2006

The first country to engage in nuclear breakout in 1998, India has deplored North Korea's test as a threat to regional peace and stability and for highlighting the dangers of clandestine proliferation. Thus does India join the ranks of the nuclear powers preaching nuclear abstinence while engaged in consenting deterrence. Others have condemned North Korea's test as "brazen," "grave" and "provocative."

It truly is remarkable how those who worship at the altar of nuclear weapons condemn others wishing to join their sect as heretics. The problem is not nuclear proliferation, but nuclear weapons. The solution therefore is not nonproliferation, but nuclear disarmament through a universal, non-discriminatory, verifiable and enforceable nuclear weapons convention, modelled on the lines of the chemical weapons convention.

For over four decades, the world has lived with five nuclear powers without a war between them. Yet today the nuclear future is less rosy than when the Non-Proliferation Treaty (NPT) was indefinitely extended in 1995.

For North Korea, nuclear weapons help to offset the loss of the former Soviet strategic counterweight, the infinitely greater economic dynamism of South Korea, and a perceptible diminution of Chinese enthusiasm for its erstwhile ally. In the past, Pyongyang has skilfully used a combination of threats, bluster and tactical retreats to win numerous economic and diplomatic concessions. It may now have played its last card. If the regime is fully quarantined and collapses, or is attacked and defeated, the resulting instability will hardly be welcomed by others in the region. Conversely, if it survives as a nuclear weapon power, South Korea, Japan and Taiwan might be tempted to follow suit. Either way, threatening storm clouds will gather pace.

I abhor rather than applaud the North Korean test. That is because I believe nuclear weapons are abhorrent, period. I argued in 1996, in a submission to the Canberra Commission, that we face four nuclear choices: the status quo, proliferation, nuclear re-armament, or abolition. Events in the intervening decade have vindicated that analysis and the Canberra Commission's conclusions.

Restoration of the 1970 NPT status quo would require a rollback of nuclear weapons by India, Pakistan, Israel and North Korea, as well as curtailment of Iran's programme. Trying to denuclearise South Asia or the Middle East is as unrealistic as demanding nuclear abolition immediately. It cannot be achieved by finger wagging at the nuclear naughtiness of recent gatecrashers into the nuclear club. The latest test, like the 11 claimed South Asian nuclear explosive tests of 1998, confirm the folly of believing – in defiance of common sense, logic and all known human history – that five powers could indefinitely retain their monopoly over one class of weapons.

Moreover, softening of the unilateral use of the military option over the past decade has given extra urgency to the motivation of would-be proliferants who fear being attacked by Washington. The Kosovo war sent a chill of apprehension down the spines of many countries that have their own secessionists. Who would be the next target of intervention by tomorrow's international moral majority? The experience of a rampant Western coalition simply bypassing the United Nations to violate the norm of non-intervention caused massive disquiet and unease and made many countries more determined to upgrade national defence.

That lesson could only have been reinforced, especially for Iran and North Korea, by the Iraq war: Saddam Hussein was attacked because he did not have nuclear weapons. Nuclear warheads and missiles suddenly acquired extra appeal as leveraging weapons.

In the case of advanced countries, the flow of enabling technologies, material and expertise in the nuclear power industry can be used, through strategic pre-positioning of materials and personnel, to build a "virtual" nuclear-weapons portfolio capable of rapid weaponization. Within the constraints of the NPT, a non-nuclear industrialized country can build the necessary infrastructure to provide it with the "surge" capacity to upgrade quickly to nuclear weapons.

Some NPT weaknesses were intentional. For example, the wording of Articles 1 and 2 deliberately permits the nuclear powers to transfer nuclear weapons to other countries (Cold War allies at the time) – that is, engage in geographical proliferation – as long as control of the weapons remained in their own hands. The popularity of regional nuclear-weapon-free zones, especially across the southern hemisphere, owed much to the desire to plug this loophole.

The wish to marry two incompatible goals – President Dwight Eisenhower's vision of "atoms for peace" and nonproliferation – produced the odd juxtaposition of Articles 3 and 4, and led in time to crises in North Korea and Iran. For nuclear energy for peaceful purposes can be pursued legitimately to the point of being a screwdriver away from a weapons capability.

Other NPT weaknesses became apparent with the benefit of hindsight. By failing to include clearly timetabled, legally binding, verifiable and enforceable disarmament commitments, it temporarily legitimized the nuclear arsenals of the N5. By relying on the promise of signatories to use nuclear materials, facilities and technology for peaceful purposes only, it empowered them to operate dangerously close to a nuclear-weapons capability. It proscribed non-nuclear states from acquiring nuclear weapons, but failed to design a strategy for dealing with non-signatory countries. It permits withdrawals much too easily.

While consciousness of the risks of nuclear weapons falling into the hands of terrorists, militant fanatics and other non-state groups has grown enormously, the collective memories of the horrors of Hiroshima and Nagasaki have begun to fade, lowering the normative barriers to the use of nuclear weapons. Because there is no standing agency or secretariat, the NPT depends on five-year review conferences for resolving implementation problems. Even these operate by the consensus rule, which does not make for decisive resolution of contentious issues.

If the NPT status quo is already history, and the risks of arms control reverses and proliferation are real, then we must either accept a world of more nuclear weapons and more nuclear powers, or move to a nuclear-weapon-free world. There is no third way.

It is difficult to convince some of the futility of nuclear weapons when all who have such weapons demonstrate their continuing utility by keeping them. The preaching of exhortations and the coercion of sanctions need to be buttressed with the force of example. The case for independent British and French nuclear deterrent forces is not compelling. Another circuit breaker in the countervailing nuclear-weapons capability spiral is the United States. Given its overwhelming military dominance with conventional arsenals, if its case to retain nuclear weapons is persuasive, then it should be even more persuasive for those countries that live in insecure neighbourhoods and lack the panoply of conventional military tools, underpinned by technological superiority, available to Washington.

Also, the best way to keep nasty weapons out of the hands of nasty groups is to keep them out of the hands of governments.

The NPT is tied to a frozen international power structure decades out of date. It became dangerously fragile because of the vertical proliferation of the nuclear powers for two decades, before they reconstructed the structure of cooperation in nuclear peace, called a halt to their proliferating arsenals, and began progressively to dismantle them under the virtuous cycle of mutually reinforcing unilateral, bilateral and multilateral arms control agreements and policies.

The road towards the nuclear-free destination includes still deeper reductions in nuclear arsenals; further constraints on the extra-territorial deployment of nuclear weapons; the entry into force of the Comprehensive Test Ban Treaty; bans on missile test flights and on the production of fissile materials; and de-alerting and de-mating of nuclear forces, warheads and missiles.

Such scenarios typically provoke dismissive comments from so-called "realists." Realistically speaking, is there another option beyond those identified here? If not, then which is the most preferred option? As with Winston Churchill's famous aphorism on democracy, the abolitionist option may well be unrealistic; all other conceivable options are even less realistic as strategies of security and survival.

The only guarantee against the threat of nuclear war is the complete elimination of nuclear weapons. In most contexts, a step-by-step approach is the best policy. Such caution can be fatal if the need is to cross a chasm. In the case of nuclear weapons, the chasm over which we must leap is the belief that world security can rest on weapons of total insecurity.

60

To feel conviction is not enough: Know the goals of military intervention

The Japan Times, 20 November 2006

In a *Washington Post* article reprinted in these pages on 10 October, "The humanitarian war myth," Eric Posner writes: "If the United Nations were to have its way, the Iraqi debacle would be just the first in a series of such wars – the effect of a well-meaning but ill-considered effort to make humanitarian intervention obligatory as a matter of international law. Today Iraq, tomorrow Darfur."

Not so.

Later he writes: "humanitarian war is an oxymoron."

Just so.

The International Commission on Intervention and State Sovereignty (ICISS) was the midwife to "the responsibility to protect" precisely because we recognized "humanitarian intervention" to be an oxymoron. It is not obvious that Posner read our slim report before proceeding to criticize its main conclusions.

In using Iraq to attack the new norm, Posner sets up a straw target. Most ICISS commissioners argued that Iraq did not meet our threshold criteria; some of us said so publicly in 2003.

Our choice of "responsibility" over "duty" flowed in part from the wish to indicate a moral but not legal obligation. We concluded that actual decisions will always be based on political judgments to meet specific contingencies case by case.

Still, the fact is that our ability and tools to act beyond our borders have increased tremendously. This greatly increases demands and expectations "to do something." Darfur is indeed the current poster case for this. It meets all our threshold criteria for the international community to shoulder its responsibility to protect.

But we also put in another essential principle: before undertaking military intervention, be confident of reasonable prospects for success in the mission. Given Sudan's size and regional geopolitics, this is a big problem in Darfur. By its very nature, including unpredictability, unintended consequences and the risk to innocent civilians caught in the crossfire, warfare is inherently brutal: nothing humanitarian about the means.

The ethic of conviction, which impels us to act, must be balanced by the equally compelling ethic of responsibility, which requires us to weigh moral action against the pragmatism of consequences.

Still, the fundamental question cannot be avoided. Under what circumstances is the use of force necessary to provide effective international humanitarian protection to at-risk populations without the consent of their own government?

Without the responsibility to protect norm and principles, the intervention is more likely to be ad hoc, unilateral, self-interested and deeply divisive. With the norm and principles agreed to in advance, military action is more likely to be rules-based, multilateral, disinterested and consensual.

Consider an analogy from health policy. Rapid advances in medical technology have greatly expanded the range, accuracy and number of surgical interventions. With enhanced capacity and increased tools have come more choices that have to be made, often involving philosophical, ethical, political and legal dilemmas. The idea of simply standing by and letting nature take its course is no longer acceptable. Parents can now be taken to court for criminal negligence of children's health.

Similarly, calls for military intervention happen. War is the use of force by enemy armies: us against them. It is by no means obsolete. But states can no longer use force as and when they want, either domestically or internationally.

Collective security requires the use of force by the community of states against an aggressor: all against one. It has proven illusory.

Peacekeeping operations insert neutral and lightly armed third-country soldiers as a physical buffer between enemy combatants who have agreed to a ceasefire. "Humanitarian intervention" is the use of force by outsiders for the protection of victims of atrocities inside sovereign territory.

In the 1990s, conscience-shocking atrocities in Somalia, Rwanda, Srebrenica and East Timor revealed a dangerous gap between the codified best practice of international behaviour in the UN Charter and the distressing state of affairs in the real world.

Rwanda in 1994 caused lasting damage to basic human ideals and UN credibility when we refused to stop, as we could have, a three-month genocide that killed 800,000 people.

Kosovo in 1999 gravely damaged UN credibility and fractured international opinion when the North Atlantic Treaty Organization intervened without UN authorization.

ICISS held that while the state has the default responsibility to protect its people, a residual responsibility also rests with the broader international community. This is activated when a particular state is either unwilling or unable to honour its responsibility to protect; or is itself the perpetrator of atrocity crimes.

The goal of protective intervention is never to wage war on a state to destroy it and eliminate its statehood, but always to protect victims of atrocities inside the state, embed the protection in reconstituted institutions after the intervention, and then withdraw all foreign troops.

Military intervention, even for humanitarian purposes, is a polite euphemism for the use of deadly force on a massive scale. Even when there is agreement that intervention may be necessary to protect innocent people from life-threatening danger by interposing an outside force between actual or apprehended victims and perpetrators, key questions remain about agency, lawfulness and legitimacy.

Based on the pragmatism of consequences as much as legal doctrine, ICISS concluded that there is no substitute for the United Nations as the authorizing agent.

Iraq reinforces the lesson that the sense of moral outrage provoked by humanitarian atrocities must be tempered by an appreciation of the limits of power, a concern for international institution-building and institution-wrecking, and sensitivity to the law of unintended and perverse consequences.

Acceptance of the responsibility-to-protect-norm no more guarantees military intervention than its non-existence had foreclosed it as a tool of statecraft. But, by shaping the calculation of the balance of interests, the norm makes it modestly more rather than less likely that victims will not be callously abandoned. We are indeed our brothers' and sisters' keepers.

61

What Annan has contributed to world

The Daily Yomiuri, 26 December 2006

If a week is a long time in national politics, then a decade is an eternity in international politics. The world has witnessed many profound changes in the ten turbulent years of Kofi Annan's term as secretary-general of the United Nations. Many – but not all – were for the good.

Thus, he oversaw an explosion in UN peace operations as testament to the numerous demands and expectations on the organization, yet many operations were dogged by charges of ineffectualness, financial corruption and sexual exploitation.

For some, Annan's legacy is indelibly stained by the horrors of Rwanda, Srebrenica and the oil-for-food scandal. For others, the tragedy of Iraq happened on his watch. Certainly, he must accept some blame for management lapses and bad judgment calls. Yet as the inquiry into the Australian Wheat Board's role in Iraqi sanctions-busting proved conclusively, the major sins of commission and omission, whether intentional or incidental, were committed by national governments, including members of the Security Council, not UN officials. If the Security Council is divided, the secretary-general cannot be an alternate locus of international diplomacy. If it is united, he cannot be an alternative focus of international dissent.

A central challenge that Annan was not able to meet successfully in every instance will continue to confront his successor: how to combine the United Nations' unique legitimacy and international authority with the United States' global reach and power. Washington too must augment its waning power with the United Nations' force-multiplying international legitimacy.

Annan's most precious legacy will probably be the elevation of human rights and humanitarian protection as a central plank of UN concern, spurred by the shocking failures of Rwanda and the Balkans. With the decline in interstate wars, the primary responsibility for maintaining international peace and security in practice translates into tackling internal armed conflicts. The world has made significant progress in criminalizing atrocity crimes and enhancing the prospects of holding perpetrators to international account. The confidence of sovereign impunity that perpetrators of atrocities enjoyed has softened, if not entirely disappeared. Serbia's Slobodan Milosevic and Chile's Augusto Pinochet may have cheated criminal conviction, but the circumstances of their deaths would not have been of their own choosing.

The new norm of the responsibility to protect, championed by Annan, captures the convergence of some significant trends in world affairs. Previously, there were few restrictions on the right of states to use force within and across borders. Our understanding and appreciation of human rights and commitment to their promotion and protection have deepened and broadened. The vocabulary of democracy, good governance and human rights has become the language of choice in international discourse.

Because human rights champions the cause of the rights and dignity of individual human beings, it is entirely fitting that the great champions of the human rights and international humanitarian law movements were such giants of individuals as Raphael Lemkin, who brought the Genocide Convention into being, Peter Benenson, who founded Amnesty International, and Henri Dunant, who started the Red Cross.

Their examples demonstrate, powerfully, that the chief impulse to human rights is the recognition that every human being is deserving of equal moral consideration. It is an acceptance of a duty of care by those living in safety towards those trapped in zones of danger. The United Nations' normative mandates on security, development and human rights alike embody this powerful intuition.

Over time, the chief threats to international security have come from violent eruptions of crises within states, including civil wars, while the goals of promoting human rights and democratic governance, protecting civilian victims of humanitarian atrocities and punishing governmental perpetrators of mass crimes have become more important. Because of the changing nature and victims of armed conflict from soldiers to civilians, including through excess deaths caused by conflict-related disease and starvation, the need for clarity, consistency and reliability in the use of force for civilian protection lies at the heart of the United Nations' core security mandate.

The UN record of policy innovation, conceptual advances, institutional adaptation and organizational learning under Annan has been underappreciated. We have seen this over the last decade with respect to peace operations, human security and human rights, atrocity crimes and international criminal justice, smart sanctions and what Annan describes as particularly precious to him – the responsibility to protect innocent civilians caught in the crossfire and victims of atrocity crimes.

Some argue that the UN Charter was written in another age for another world. For many others, it remains vitally relevant. It is the framework within which the scattered and divided fragments of humanity come together to look for solutions without passports to problems without borders.

Many of the most intractable problems are global in scope and will most likely require concerted multilateral action that is also global in its reach. But the policy authority for tackling them remains vested in states, and the competence to mobilize the resources needed for tackling them is also vested in states. This strategic disconnect goes some way to explaining the United Nations' recurrent difficulties on many fronts and the often fitful nature of its responses. How Ban Ki-moon, Annan's successor, handles it will help to determine his legacy in turn.

The temper of the times condition expectations of the role of the UN secretary-general. The changing contours of world politics provide the context in which opportunities, requirements and constraints on the scope for UN role and independent action by the secretary-general are shaped. For example, Annan is personally credited with reaching out to the business sector through his Global Compact that seeks to instil civic virtue in the global marketplace, as well as to civil society representatives who have found the United Nations a far more hospitable place under his stewardship.

Yet both of these were made possible by major changes in a much larger context. The end of the Cold War marked the triumph of liberal economics over the command economy and the concurrent rise of civil society activism within and across borders. This was reflected in the abatement of reflexive hostility to market capitalism and nongovernmental activism by many UN member states. Annan's genius lay in channelling the historic ideational transformations into new institutional linkages. Ban must remain hospitable to partnerships with these vital actors in driving desirable changes and delivering growth, services and security in the field.

The United Nations' very strength as the common meeting house of all the world's countries is a major source of weakness with respect to efficient decision-making. Even so, we must never fall victim to the soft bigotry of low expectations. Rather, we must always hold the organization to the more exacting standard of exalted expectations. That is the final tribute to a fundamentally decent man with generous instincts who raised the bar of people's aspirations, but whose generous interpretations of the conduct of others sometimes proved sadly misplaced.

Index of names